BEYOND GENESIS

BEYOND GENESIS

THE UNTOLD STORY OF MAN'S ORIGINS

Allen Epling

Library of Congress Number:		2005910583
ISBN:	Hardcover	1-4257-0415-8
	Softcover	1-4257-0414-X

To order additional copies of this book, contact:
Xlibris Corporation
1-888-795-4274
www.Xlibris.com
Orders@Xlibris.com
32435

CONTENTS

I would like to dedicate this book to my wife, Marie, who was persistent in pushing me to write it, and my father, Phillip K. Epling, a writer and author far beyond my equal.

Introduction

It seems a little strange that in the age of enlightenment and understanding that we are enjoying, that there should be such a bitter debate over the creation of man in our schools and religious institutions. I'm disappointed at the resistance of either side to considering alternative solutions. People of faith have had their traditional views of this subject challenged by the scientific discoveries of the last two centuries, but even in the face of irrefutable evidence of such subjects as the age of the Earth, they refuse to consider the possibility that if indeed the Bible is true and infallible, maybe it is a failure of their interpretation of the Bible that is the problem.

This book explores how the Bible, specifically the book of Genesis, can be believed and still be compatible with our knowledge of science and history. In it you will find many ideas that go against popular belief in both the religious and the scientific communities. You will find that these ideas are logical and by accepting them, all the mysteries of Genesis suddenly become clear. You will also find that most of the confusion about Genesis and its "myths" was caused by the mis-translation of only one word, a word that in the Hebrew language had a double meaning.

Fundamentalist ministers continue to insist on a "literal" interpretation of the Bible, and preach from the pulpit consistently that to accept the science version of these controversial subjects is to go against God Himself. Maybe it is because no one has yet offered an acceptable "literal" interpretation that holds true to the message of the Bible

Alternately, the academic community is equally convinced that the Bible is filled with, and is about, superstition and myths, and that there is nothing of value in the Bible to consider as important information. They will argue passionately with anyone who advocates accepting any part of it as being true. Some college and university professors go so far as to penalize students for using material from the Bible in research papers, a practice I consider deplorable for any academician worthy of the title.

Students should have the right to use *any* source to support a hypothesis without being threatened by an instructor's anti-religious bias.

Both views are wrong and, in my opinion, are born out of ignorance. I have struggled with these subjects since childhood and have yet to find any area of science that is incompatible with the Bible if a person is willing to apply a little effort and imagination to explain and develop an adjusted interpretation.

Some will argue that I am not reading the Bible literally, but as I will show later, there is no such thing as a literal interpretation of what we commonly call the Bible because they are all translations of the original, the five books of Moses as presented on Mt. Sinai. It is my goal to adhere as closely as possible to a very "literal" explanation of the events in the book of Genesis by referring not to "translations" of this Bible, but to the only literal version that ever existed, the one just referred to. All other versions are imperfect translations that someone had to "interpret" in order to convert them from the original Hebrew to another language. Some will say that the translations themselves were divinely inspired. If that is true then why do we have so many different versions of a divinely inspired document?

Many religious people feel that every new science discovery seems to threaten the existence of God. Science deals only with physical laws and the structure of the universe. My belief in God is based on the assumption that He created all that we are studying in science and is outside the problem. He can never be proven or disproved by science because science deals only with physics and God is not physical. A belief that there is a God has to be based on *faith* in His existence.

It may seem a little odd for some readers that I speak of people, places and events that they have always thought of as myths or legends, as if they were real. I hope that they endure these feelings and read on, to allow me to qualify these statements with support and justifications.

I have tried to present the reader with what I think is a new perspective on man's history and development, but in a way that is logical, supported with evidence, and sometimes, proofs. The result is a story that flows logically from beginning to end, with admittedly, some speculation on my part, but only when the evidence, resulting historical data, and the Bible supports it.

To some readers it may seem that this book is religious in nature, and I respect the right of everyone to believe as they choose, but this book is about the history of man in that his very early history is not determined with any degree of certainty in the scientific world and the book of Genesis does provide an explanation. My reason for writing this book is to offer reasons to believe that the accounts in Genesis are true, and some reasonable explanations for some of the more mysterious gaps in our history that may have a religious connection. If I have done that without insulting the reader's intelligence, then I have succeeded.

Chapter One

THE FIRST MAN

When I began writing this book, I had the ambitious, but sincere goal of trying to explain some of the "myths" of the book of Genesis, dealing with each event as a separate story, and a separate project. The one basic assumption I wanted to adhere to throughout the book was that the book of Genesis was historically accurate, but that our interpretation of the events described by it was not accurate. I believed that if we could only interpret it correctly, it would fit with what we know to be true according to scientific data.

As the narrative progressed, I started to feel that, instead of my determining the course of the book; the book was pulling me in a direction different from the path I had originally set out to cover. Separate, seemingly unrelated events were coming together into a storyline that had previously gone unnoticed through the ages. The great events of Genesis were all connected by a common theme that is not casually revealed but was definitely present in the beginning, in the garden.

Earlier Biblical scholars, who did not have the benefit of modern research and new knowledge that has just recently come to light, had missed it. The act of writing about it was revealing details to me that would help explain some of those mysteries, such as the flood of Noah, a better understanding of why the world had to be destroyed, the possibility of using DNA to find out who the REAL Adam was, the unexplained explosion of technology around 2200 BC, and the central reason for everything that happened in the book of Genesis. I sensed the undercurrent of a story that had remained hidden and untold until such a time when we were ready to accept and understand it. That time appeared to be the present. It seemed that the entire book of Genesis was playing out on a much grander scale than I had imagined.

If someone said to you that every word of the book of Genesis in the Old Testament is an accurate historical description of what happened between 3000 and 6000 years ago most likely you would say "It's just not possible"? There may even be some people of faith who would agree. Some have already concluded that the stories were either exaggerated tales or were misunderstood by the human writers of the books. Yet many good people of faith feel that the book is inspired, and struggle to hold on to the idea that the stories of the flood, and other fantastic tales that were told to them in Sunday school are true and accurate.

Those who accept the standard "intellectually elite" position on evolution would say that the truth lies in the archeology and abundant physical evidence that man began to emerge from the animal kingdom around 2 million years ago.

What if I said to you that both groups are right and that there is a way to explain how both versions of man's creation could be true without violating the truth of the Bible? Is it possible that there is an explanation that would satisfy anyone who is searching for the truth and has an open mind? Most likely you would have serious doubts about any hypothesis or explanation that tried to cover so much ground.

I have always held to the belief that every word in the Book of Genesis is both true and accurate. Like others, I had problems relating the incredible "stories" I heard in Sunday school, to what I was taught to be true in my studies of science and history. Instead of falling on one side of the fence or the other as usually happens in an issue so divided, I decided to reserve final judgment until enough evidence could be gathered to reconcile the issue. I was certain that neither side knew all there was to know on the subject. I had faith that the ingenuity of man would someday shed light on this and all other mysteries. Surely a way could be found to "explain" the book of Genesis without violating either the laws of God or the physical laws of the universe. It seemed to me that there was enough uncertainty in both arguments to allow for re-interpretation of the "facts".

I get very upset when someone of high academic or religious standing says "The Bible is not to be used as a history book". I believe that they have given up too soon. Contrary to the position that some authors have taken, that Genesis is simply a beautiful allegory, I don't believe God wrote the book of Genesis just to make a beautiful story for our entertainment! Either it is true and accurate or it is false. Truth does not belong exclusively to a category of science or religion. The truth, like water, will find its own level wherever it falls.

In the process of writing this book, which began as a collection of notes gathered from years of pondering the "mysteries" of the Old Testament, I stumbled, either accidentally or with some "outside help", upon some insights, that we will cover later, which could well explain these stories logically, and reconcile the differences between the "science" version of the creation of man and the Genesis version. I always knew that there were many things that I couldn't explain, but I had faith that in time the truth would reveal itself either through new discoveries or more informed insight.

It has to be understood by the reader that certain "interpretations" of facts will have to be radically changed for this to work, because many very intelligent people have worked on this problem over the last century and failed. The reason for this failure is two-fold. Either they didn't have the courage to explore alternate interpretations of the Bible for fear of breaking tradition, or lacked the imagination to see them.

To accomplish this task, some of my most cherished ideas of religious tradition had to give way to new perspectives that have become possible only in the last 30 years. I reluctantly gave up these views only when I realized the evidence was overwhelmingly against them and that it was possible that the traditional interpretation wasn't what the original scriptures said anyway. Alternately, some of the most respected and accepted opinions of science had to be compromised to some extent to allow for a hypothesis that proposes what most scientists find objectionable, that the Bible really is a true and accurate record of history.

There is a familiar saying that, *"If you continue to do as you have always done, you can expect to get what you've always gotten."*

Any explanation that would bring together such opposing views of man and his role in the universe as science and religion, would naturally have to be something we have never imagined or tried before, else we would "get what we have always gotten".

What happened next was unexpected to say the least. If my understanding of the story that was unfolding before me was true, it would dramatically change our perception of who we are and how "modern" man came to be. I have to confess that what I experienced internally was fear. *Fear that the story was bigger than my ability to tell it.*

Thus begins a story about God and His creation that, since writing it, I have felt even more, that I have stumbled onto the REAL truth about what happened 6000 years ago when man emerged, almost overnight, out of the darkness of ignorance into the light of an age of civilization and reason.

Each of the following "insights" will be discussed in-depth in later chapters.

The first "breakthrough", or insight came as I was writing about the Garden of Eden and its relationship to the Creation and all subsequent events. This idea was only the beginning but probably is the one that set the tone for all that follows.

INSIGHT #1: The first two chapters of Genesis describe two different events, separated in time by billions of years.

When the idea first occurred to me, I re-examined my understanding of those events. I was suddenly stunned with a 'What if . . ." type of thought process that demanded a closer look to see if scriptures that followed supported this idea all along but we just didn't notice it.

What if the book of Genesis, chapters 1 and 2, was describing two different events separated by a great span of time? Scholars have wondered for a long time why the creation story was repeated starting in Genesis 2:4 and have debated the reason for centuries. We have always assumed that the two chapters were the same event, but that the second account in chapter 2 was simply a closer look at the creation of Man. What if the events in Chapter 1 concerning the creation of the heavens and the Earth took place billions of years ago, and the events of Chapter 2 actually took place only 6000 years ago as a second "creation" event? If true, then Genesis 1 and 2 seem to reflect the modern scientific view of creation while Genesis 2 describes the traditional religious view. The science community insists that universe is over 12 billion years old and the Earth is 4.5 billion years old, while fundamentalist Christians say man and history only began 6000 years ago, according to the Bible. Interpreting chapters 1 and 2 this way seems to say that both are right. Perhaps the answer was before us all along.

If that is true, then Adam would truly be the first man by the Bible's definition and still allow for the existence of all the creatures described in our science books as having evolved, *including a creature the science books call "early man"*.

Of course the argument the religious right would use against this is that the Bible talks of the creation taking 6 days. There is a flood of irrefutable evidence that all of creation is billions of years old. The "days" mentioned in the Bible were spoken of as a time period before there was a "day" to measure it by. We now define a day as the time it takes for the Earth to rotate once. What was the length of a day before man defined it this way? Using that as the standard, a day could have been any period of time before the Earth existed. Even the Bible supports this idea by declaring in several places that God's time is not the same as man's time.

At this point I began to understand another important concept.

INSIGHT #2: There existed a primitive creature that the science community calls "man", before Adam, that lived in great numbers around the world, outside of Eden.

This thought-provoking, and perhaps the most controversial proposal, is that there was a form of man that existed for millennia on this earth before Adam and that the man spoken of by the Bible in the Garden of Eden and afterward, was not the same creature as the man we read about in our science books about that time. They were separate species and lived independently in different areas of the world. If we read the Bible "literally", Man was created from the dust of Eden, not as a preexisting creature. Throughout our history we have taken the name for our species, man, from the Bible, and only in the last 150 years has the science community taken that term and applied it to a creature that did not originate in the Garden of Eden. Our science textbooks speak of man as the creature that was born out of evolutionary processes two million years ago.

Is it possible that the two creatures may not be one and the same? Is it also possible that, since we don't have all the characteristics that Adam had, "modern man" as we know him didn't exist until around 5000 years ago when the descendants of Adam (and Noah) mixed with primitive "man" who was already here, and created a new species. That new species is us, or modern man according to the science books.

It is clear from the Bible that we are different from Adam, and I believe that we are also different from the species of man described in our classrooms as Homo sapiens, the man who dominated the Earth around 10,000 B. C. Could it be that the conflict between creationism and evolution is simply a matter of definitions, that the term "Man" is used to apply to two different creatures and depends on whose definition you accept.

We speak of "Man" today as if everything that ever lived that walked upright and made tools was "man". That is the modern view. We have to realize that when the Bible speaks of "man" it is only referring to someone who is a descendent of Adam. Biblical scholars have talked of a "divine spark" that God put in Adam that is present in everyone who is a descendent of him. Genesis calls it the "Breath of Life". Its very possible that the "divine spark" is a genetic signature that becomes a part of everyone that is a descendant of Adam, and that will only be discovered when we are able to fully understand the entire genetic code of the human race.

If we take the view that the term "man" can apply to two different creatures that were very different from each other, but lived in the same period of time, all kinds of possibilities open up and some of the greatest mysteries of the Bible are "solved"

When Genesis 4: verses 16 and 17 state that Cain left Eden and took a wife, we now have an explanation for where she came from. The "man", Cain, the Bible refers to, took a wife from among the creatures that our science books call "man". These creatures look very much like modern man but lacked the genetic "Breath of Life" that God implanted in Adam. The passage above is conspicuous by its lack of information as to where the wife came from and does not say that she was of Adam, perhaps by design.

The scriptures that follow support this theory. Genesis 4:20-24 gives in detail the contributions that Cain's descendants make to later history, such as music, iron and metalworking, etc. If all of his descendants had perished in the flood, this would have been unimportant and meaningless, as their work would have perished with them. Why bother to include this as part of the narrative if it is irrelevant or untrue?

The truth is that after Cain left Eden to dwell among the "primitive" man of our science textbooks, his descendants were spared the catastrophe of the flood, which was confined to the area called Eden. As I will show in detail later this was "the world" that was destroyed and not the whole planet Earth. God did truly destroy "man whom I have created" because the creatures living outside of Eden were not considered to be "man" by God, and were not destroyed. The phrase "that I have created" is referring to only the creation in the Garden of Eden.

The "other" men are the creatures referred to in Genesis 1:26 when God said "Let us make man in our image". This creature would eventually become man by God's plan but was only the first step in the process of man's creation. The final phase of this plan would take place when Adam's descendants mixed his genes with those of this creature. Adam was not this man but the man God created from dust in the garden.

Stated another way, when the Bible says Adam was the first man, it is using God's definition of Man as created in the garden, and is correct, *by definition*. By this standard, Adam didn't even have to look like us to be "Man". When our children read about "early man" in their science books, and those books say that the first man began about two million years ago, they are accepting science's definition of "man", not God's. Who then was the "true" Man if they were different? My argument is that both groups are right within the boundaries of their *definitions* of "man".

As we shall see later, they were two very different creatures, both of which had some of the features of modern man, but in some ways both were very different from man today. We read about Adam and his immediate descendents and think of them as normal, like you and me. Read Genesis more carefully concerning their characteristics and you will see that they were not like you and me. Specifically, the race of man from Adam to Noah and his immediate descendents was a very unusual "man" by todays, or any period's standards, in his longevity, immunity to disease, his ability to communicate with God, and other characteristics we will go into later.

If we accept the premise that God had something special intended for the "primitive" man that existed outside the garden, then this era suddenly becomes tremendously important. The period between the end of the Flood and the beginning of civilization was starting to take on a complexity and character that could legitimately be called a blueprint for the future of Man

What happened then could not have succeeded without a great deal of coordination and forethought as to how it would be implemented. Its scope was to include every race and people on the planet.

The plan, at least in part, began when God said, "Let us create man in our image". At that time there was no creature that resembled modern man alive. Science tells us that a creature they call Australopithecus suddenly appeared and through the process of evolution and in the millennia of time developed into a form of man that resembled modern man. God's plan was to create a superior human being called Adam, instruct him to multiply and "replenish" the Earth, so that in time his descendants would mix with the inferior habitants of this world to produce a race of beings that would develop a technological society and arrive at the point we now enjoy and know as the modern world. A secondary meaning for the word replenish is to "replace". The word replenish, as used here, was a command to re-populate the earth with a new kind of man that was to *replace* the previous or primitive race that descended from Australopithecus. Re-populate means that there was something before man.

The reason for this plan, and the end result would be a large enough population of this "modern man", as we now call him, from which to extract only those who are worthy to enter into what the Bible calls "The Kingdom of God".

Jesus consistently referred to this domain and emphasized that it required not only understanding but also a sensitivity and grasp of morals that the primitive man could never have achieved. It would be hard to see how anyone could argue how His message of "Love thy neighbor, and even thy enemy" could have impacted the world of man 10,000 years ago, yet this simple phrase is still affecting man's thinking and is debated today. This is proof that something in man had changed.

Misinterpretations of the message have admittedly resulted in some disastrously misguided efforts such as the Spanish inquisition, the Crusades, and the Salem witch trials. This is an indication that some of the primitive man who lacked understanding of the "love" message is still present in all of us.

This coordinated effort to introduce civilization and reason to the world of man will never appear in any school textbook because it would support the "religious" view of creation. The official position of the science community is still that civilization and progress all happened by accident through a few key developments in agriculture. They admit that these are still a puzzle, and are at a loss to explain the explosion of knowledge and language that took place just after the time of the flood, around 4500 years ago. During this period, man invented language, written alphabets, studied mathematics, learned to smelt iron, and constructed the first cities made of bricks. *All of this occurred within a space of only 300 years!*

When the "Eden" man mixed with "primitive man" after the flood, the very nature of man as a species was changed as the genes of these "enhanced humans', direct descendants of Adam, were assimilated into the gene pool of the existing creatures that science calls 'man'. The result was a new form of man that was intelligent, artistic, and very creative. The bipedal hominid of our science books that had roamed the Earth for more than two million years was now changed to be a moral creature with the "divine spark", at least in theory, if not in practice.

At this point a realization set in for what was becoming clearer with each chapter. I developed a deeper appreciation of the fact that everyone walking around on the Earth today has some of the genes, and is a descendant of, a real person named Adam. And, since those genes came directly from God, we could even call ourselves "children of God". We will find out later that some individuals even assigned an element of "divinity" to that title. Also, as "children of God" we acquired a "right of inheritance". That right, as is true in all inheritances, is only valid if we claim it.

That right of inheritance makes us eligible for consideration to become members of the "Kingdom of God". This helps to explain the verse in John 1: 12 and 13 in the New Testament concerning our right to be called "Sons of God". It also confirms that every individual is special and is important to God because we all have his stamp, or seal of ownership, within us. *I believe that this stamp, or brand, of God is contained in our DNA.*

Is it possible that the writers of the New Testament had access to knowledge of this part of our history that we have not yet realized? There are several instances of the word "mystery" or "mysteries" being used in the New Testament to refer to knowledge that we will have at some point in the future.

The apostle Paul is very vague in a passage that has intrigued Bible scholars for centuries concerning the physical man and spiritual man. This is contained in Corinthians 2:14, "for the natural man received not the things of the spirit of God: for they are foolishness unto him . . .".

This is followed up by even more specific references to *two* kinds of Man in chapter 15:47, "The first man is from the earth, a man of dust. The second man is from heaven . . . Just as we have born the image of the man of dust, we will also bear the image of the man of heaven". We could easily substitute the word "genes" for the word "image" in this statement, and retain the same meaning. This is a very powerful and timely statement from someone who had no knowledge of genetics. If the ideas presented in this manuscript are true then we all DO bear the *genetic* image of both the primitive man of the science books as well as the image of the first man, Adam, who, because God "breathed the spirit of life into him", is the only one who can legitimately be called a "man of heaven".

There was at this time available to Paul, a library in Egypt, at Alexandria, which contained the sum of all knowledge then known in the ancient world. Perhaps Paul, being a very learned and literate person from that period, had read from texts that were stored in this library. Perhaps he acquired greater knowledge of man's history after his conversion to Christianity. It is well known that all of the written documents concerning mankind's history from the beginning of written language were stored in this library, which was later destroyed by the Romans. What could we have learned about our early history if those documents had survived to this day? Would we have learned that the flood story in the Bible was true and accurate? Would they tell of the origin of the "mythical" Gods who lifted the ancient civilizations, like Greece, out of the Stone Age? Would we now have a greater appreciation of the Old Testament accuracy if those texts could corroborate its authenticity?

I was now starting to comprehend the importance of the fact that all of the significant events that transformed man from a backward nomadic existence to a literate, cultured, citizen with an urban lifestyle, took place in a very small region of the world between 2200 and 2500 BC, a very short time period in which Man and his world were re-invented and set on a course to become what it is today.

INSIGHT #3: The flood of Noah was a local event, confined to a large area called EDEN. Throughout the book of Genesis before chapter 9, this area was referred to as "the world"

As this document began to take shape new evidence was just coming to light concerning the flood of Noah. This would later become a crucial piece in the puzzle. It led to a new perspective on that event that helped me to understand much better how and why it happened. I started to fully appreciate the tremendous effect it had on the Earth and the future of Man. A full explanation of this event is given in a later chapter.

Even more important to our present society and civilization, it was becoming clear for the first time the staggering importance of the period and the events that took place just after the flood of Noah. This was the period that cast the mold for modern civilization.

INSIGHT #4: The phrase "His way" as used in Genesis 6:12 should be taken to mean His plan, or blueprint for man's development.

When Adam and Eve were expelled from the Garden of Eden, they were unprotected from the elements. Interestingly, it is at this time that the Bible gives us one of the most puzzling passages in the entire book. Genesis 6:1-7 describes beings coming from Heaven who take wives of the daughters of Man. This results in offspring that are described as "giants", who are obviously very different from the race begun by Adam. Because of this genetic corruption of Adam's line God declares in no uncertain terms "I will destroy man whom I have created from the face of the Earth . . . for all flesh had corrupted His WAY on the face of the Earth".

In reading the passage in Genesis 6:12 that said "God's way was corrupted" I saw something else that had been passed over. The choosing of the word "way" for this passage is a little strange. When we "have our way" it usually means that we know where we are going. In other words, God had a preconceived plan that was being violated. God didn't just create the world and put man in it just to see what would develop.

When I thought about that possibility, the events that followed made more sense than before, when we simply thought the word "way" meant His creation.

This significant use of the word "way" is a subtle change that has never been truly recognized, but is extremely important here. The phrase *"His Way"* did not mean His *"Will"*, or His *"creation"*, as we usually interpret it, but was specifically referring to *a blueprint for man's development*. The word "way" is derived from a word meaning a "road" or highway such as "The Apian Way". All roads lead to somewhere that is predetermined. **God's WAY** was the plan He had set in motion for man and the Earth, even before He began the Garden project.

It became a statement that God had a plan for man that went beyond just creating him and populating the Earth. It has generally been accepted that the reason God created Man was that "He desired companionship", or "He wanted our love". While these arguments may be true, they are speculative because we cannot really determine from the Bible why God created the human race. It could also be that God had more specific plans for man that went well beyond anything we could have imagined.

What if man was created for a different reason that we have not yet realized? Until this age of information provided the tools, the knowledge, and the insight to discern it, it has remained hidden from our view. This makes the statement in Genesis that "His way was corrupted upon the Earth . . ." a much more powerful message than the traditional interpretation that He was just angry that His creation had been defiled. Not only was He angry concerning man's sinful behavior but their actions were also tearing down the wonderfully complex plan He had begun to execute in the Garden, for the benefit of all Mankind.

With that in mind a story began to play out in my imagination as the book of Genesis started to take on a new life that made more sense in our modern world. I started to realize that a picture was forming of a very detailed and complete story about God's purpose for man on the Earth that began long ago at the foundation of the world, and is still coming together in our present time.

I began to see our present world as not being so separated from the world of 6000 years ago, as the events described in Genesis suddenly became very real.

It is hard today for us to relate to a backward society, like the one that existed at that time, when we are surrounded by creations of our own, the technology and culture that runs our society and our lives. I thought about the intelligence and technology that must have been involved in the creation of The Garden of Eden, and that maybe it still existed on Earth immediately before the flood of Noah. Could it be that the technology that we have today is not entirely the result of our genius, but was predestined to happen long ago, in the time when the future of man was being molded?

For some reason, that we can only speculate about, God began, as the Bible states, at the "foundation of the world", with his plan for mankind, a time when science tells us was about 4.5 billion years ago, when the earth was "gathered together" from the dust that circled a new sun. He made a deliberate and planned decision to return to a specific time in its development, 6000 years ago, to continue and complete its final phase.

Sometimes the best way to test a hypothesis is to try on the idea, like trying on a coat, and see if there is any contradictory evidence or something that doesn't "fit". Lacking this you then examine all the available remaining evidence to see if it supports and 'reads' as if your original assumption is true. If that test proves correct you sometimes find that what remains is an idea that fits your hypothesis like a glove. That was the case here.

This new hypothesis required accepting some basic assumptions that will be described later, assumptions that would go against centuries of tradition, and go against what many had accepted as truth all their lives. The result was a story that was continuous and logical, and had a much more important message for our generation than we had realized.

When the basic form of the plan was first realized, I started to research the hypothesis, looking for supporting evidence. Pieces of the puzzle began to come together, faster than I had expected. With every chapter and idea would come new insight that explained scripture that had been a mystery since I was very young. There had to be a reason that the story was coming together so well.

INSIGHT #5: It was Noah's descendents who were responsible for the myths of "Gods" in all the great civilizations of the world.

A study of the Gods of different cultures is a part of our history that has never been given the attention it deserved by biblical and historical scholars. Perhaps it is because all historians like to think that they investigate only those ideas that are acceptable to the establishment, and a research project to study "Gods" would border on religion and superstition. Biblical researchers consider such a study as pagan and irreverent. The Bible clearly describes how the "nations" came to exist, and the role played by Noah's sons and descendants. Before there were "nations" there were only isolated colonies of nomads and people who could only struggle to hunt for or grow enough food to sustain them. Because of Noah's descendants these colonies of early humans gained knowledge and gifts of better crops, and began to build cities. Historians and science scholars like to pretend that Noah and Genesis chapter 10 never happened.

Another reason that it has not been studied more carefully is for lack of information. To write this book required accepting ideas that would provoke controversy in both the academic and the religious camps. If we are to use all the information available concerning this period in time, we have to combine the knowledge that both groups have gathered concerning the history of man. One of the problems is that we never considered is that there might have been more than one species of man, an idea that has suddenly become acceptable in light of the discovery of the "Hobbits" race in Indonesia in 2004.

The first 3 or 4 generations of Noah's descendents still had many of the traits of the pure line from Adam to Noah. They lived extremely long lives, were highly intelligent, immune to disease, and knew how to construct things no human had ever constructed before. Consider that the "other" man had a short 30 to 40 year lifespan and limited abilities, how would such a visitor as one of Noah's grandsons seem to them? He would seem to be a God in their eyes.

It would not be hard to imagine that the Greek legends of human Gods who were strong and had superhuman abilities such as Hercules, Atlas, Zeus, and others, long considered as part of Greek "mythology", were really stories about actual people who came to them as descendents of Noah. As these "super humans" inter-mixed with the primitive tribes, their offspring by mortal women would be accepted as Gods also, but only as ½ Gods, exactly as many accounts describe them, such as the epic of Gilgamesh in ancient Shumer. Gilgamesh was described in clay tablets as being only a 2/3 God. This lead to many royal lines being looked on by the people as divine.

This also explains the attempt of so many Egyptian rulers to keep the illusion alive of being divine and immortal long after these traits had been reduced through marriage and mixing with the original peoples, so as to be almost non-existent.

Had the events not taken place exactly as described here and later in this book, man today would probably still be a backward creature roaming the earth, hunting and gathering food as he did 6000 years ago, very primitive agriculture, no brick cities, and little or no written language.

Finally, but most important to today's generation, the story I am about to reveal to my readers is a continuing story. That means that it isn't finished yet. Anyone who can read will acknowledge that we are today experiencing an explosion of knowledge and enlightenment that is unparalleled in history. Yet in many ways it is very similar to what took place around 2500 B.C., just after the flood of Noah. Those events transformed man from a tribal, nomadic, subsistence way of life, into citizens of an age of urbanization and culture.

Why is that important? Because if that is true, then perhaps we too are standing on the threshold of another new age for mankind that will lift him to a higher plateau of achievement and knowledge that we can only begin to imagine.

Chapter Two

RELIGION VS SCIENCE

Since most of this book is an attempt to reconcile the differences between the scientific position on "Creationism" and the widely accepted religious views, this would be a good time to explain how we came to this point. The truth is that this battle has more to do with ego and history than intellectual prowess or faith.

Our use of computers and the internet has led to a revolution in our time that fulfills the prophesy of the book of Daniel 12:4, that "Many shall run to and fro and knowledge shall be increased". In the acquiring of that knowledge we have learned some valuable lessons concerning our interpretations of what we observe. Many scientists today have encountered barriers that defy common sense, only to find that great rewards await those who have the commitment and courage to press on beyond what their intellect tells them is possible.

Albert Einstein tried to find solutions to problems involving the speed of light and the relationship of time and space. He only succeeded when he allowed himself to venture "outside the box", and to believe in the possibility that time itself is flexible and not constant. This was an outrageous point of view to a world that was very much dedicated to the static equations of Sir Isaac Newton. The result was his famous Special Theory of Relativity.

Common sense had prevented other scientists from making that breakthrough because they could not bring themselves to accept and consider that possibility. Notice that the Bible also states that "time" is flexible in chapter 3, verse 8 of 2 Peter of the New Testament, that "a thousand years is as a day to the Lord". "Common sense" ideas can sometimes become a barrier that prevents us from seeing the truth when it goes against what we have become comfortable with.

It has been said that most people will tolerate and endure a familiar untruth, over accepting an unfamiliar truth.

26

Sadly, that is the attitude of many of the leaders in the scientific community as well as the religious. The "comfort zone" people have created for their beliefs and doctrines has taken many years to develop and any idea that changes or challenges that area of their minds immediately meets strong resistance, regardless of how strong the argument or evidence.

Many of our present ideas about the book of Genesis are rooted in centuries of thought that didn't have the benefit of the vast reservoir of knowledge that we have today. These ideas have been familiar to us all and have been accepted for so long that to many, any other explanation is heresy.

Too many religious leaders today refuse to consider any interpretation of the Bible other than the one handed down to them by tradition. Many of them aren't even aware that there was a time when church councils met to discuss and decide what was truth and what was not, and that some of the ideas about the Bible that we accept today as written in stone, were not always universally accepted by all Christians. Religion today should be so open-minded. Would God have given us the intelligence to understand and to question, if He didn't intend for us to use it to try to understand Him better? Can we have the courage to consider the possibility that *maybe the Bible really is a completely accurate historical document*? Maybe the problem is that no one has worked hard enough at trying to find an explanation that would fit both the known facts of science today and the version as recorded in Genesis.

A chasm exists today between religion and science because of events that date back to the Scopes Monkey Trial that took place in a small town in Tennessee in the 1920's. This was a trial over the dismissing of a schoolteacher for teaching that Man was a result of evolutionary forces. Because the religious group mistakenly thought that Darwin had said that Man descended from the Apes, they called it the "Monkey Trial".

Due to the bitterness with which it was debated and fought in the courtroom, and in the press afterward, religion and science were irreparably polarized. Both sides were convinced that they alone had the correct answer because of the absurd arguments used during this debate,. The science community afterward assumed a pseudo-intellectual stance and refused to touch or consider any religious issue as anything but superstition and fantasy. The religious leaders became equally convinced that to accept anything the science books taught would be to reject God. The truth is that neither group had the tools or enough information at that time to make an intelligent decision on the subject. It required an age of enlightenment, the present age of communication and computers, to clear the muddy waters.

After the event ended with a "trial by media", religious leaders would immediately try to find a "spiritual" explanation for every new science discovery that would not require a physical proof. Many Biblical "truths" were stretched in the pulpit to the point of almost breaking due to these attempts to "hang on" to the old, traditional beliefs that, in their eyes, "had to be true, "because the Bible says so, literally". Instead of taking the new evidence and adapting their "interpretations" to allow for it, there was an automatic reaction to dismiss it as heresy and anti-God. If this kind of change had not already taken place in the past in the church we would still have preachers telling their congregations that the world is flat and everything in the universe revolves around it. The church survived that transformation and only religious pride and tradition prevents it from doing so today.

No single issue has caused more strife between religion and science than the debate over creationism and evolution. Strange as it may seem to some readers, it is a conflict that exists to an extreme only in this country.

Because of Scopes Trial event the two groups were polarized to a degree in this country that is not seen in Russia or other advanced countries where many of the Bible's records are still accepted as factual history by the people, if not the state. In the countries of Armenia and Georgia of the former USSR, the people living in the area around Mt. Ararat still cling to tales of the flood and Noah's landing of the Ark on that site. Many of these people can trace their lineage and family history back to the days just after the flood, through oral tradition. With this close, direct linkage to Noah, who lived for over 900 years, could there be a connection as to why they have some of the oldest living inhabitants on the planet?

In spite of the problems just mentioned we have to recognize that we have made progress from the "official" positions of the church 500 years ago, when the world was flat and the sun revolved around the Earth. Yet Christianity and Judaism have incorporated the new findings and still survived. The fact that it has survived is proof to me that the Bible is based on a foundation of truth. The Bible is considered by most Christians to be "infallible", but what we sometimes forget is that our interpretation of the Bible is not infallible. In order to understand the truth about what happened concerning the creation of man we have to be prepared to adjust our interpretations if needed, and determine if we are reading the passages and thoughts as they were originally intended to be read.

Even though the Bible has been the most printed and read book in the history of man, there is wide disagreement over what it says in some passages. There are some who advocate a strict "literal" interpretation of the Bible. I would like to ask those individuals if they can read ancient Hebrew. The simple truth is that there is no such thing as a "literal" interpretation of the Bible. Any commentary or description of an event in the Bible involves "interpreting" something because the art of translation is imperfect and languages in general are imperfect. What many have argued as the "literal" truth of the Bible is in every case a translation of the real truth, that which was given to Moses by God on Mt. Sinai, and it wasn't written in Old English as in the King James version or modern English. All translations in print today carry the word "version" after their title. This alone should tell the reader that it is one of many translations, each of which is in some way imperfect. The only "perfect" Word was the five original books of Moses, written in Hebrew 3000 years ago.

Even if we are able to read the original Hebrew version, we have to struggle to try to determine what the author meant by certain statements because there are some Hebrew words that had double meanings. Someone had to decide which of the two meanings to accept, by the context in which it was used.

Proper credit should be given to the dedicated laborers who diligently conducted those first translations centuries ago, because they realized all too well the price of mis-interpreting even one word of the Bible. With this in mind, it is safe to say that today's Bibles are very accurate in passing on the thoughts as contained in the original Hebrew Bible, into an English version. As I will explain later however, there are a few examples of the translators, being all too human, making the wrong choice when the original word had two meanings.

If there is a good example of not being able to understand a document through a strict, literal interpretation, consider the constitution of the United States. Men are still struggling to determine what it actually says. In some legal cases, judges have to decide if the author of a law wanted it interpreted "literally" or in the spirit in which it was written. There are passages in the Bible that I believe God wanted us to read "in the spirit in which it was written" and did not intend for us to try to apply a distorted "literal" interpretation to it.

As an example of how a "literal translation" is impossible consider the reference in Revelation 7:1 to an Angel standing on the four corners of the world. Many people used that reference two centuries ago to argue against the world being round.

It has been said that communication takes place when the idea that is spoken is the same as the idea that is heard. In reading the Bible we have a tendency to sometimes "hear" what we want to hear, in spite of what is being said. If we were flexible enough to translate the original text of the Bible in so many of the different ways and versions that are in print today, we should also be flexible enough to re-interpret certain parts of the Bible if new evidence indicates a need to do so. After all, we are reading words that were originally written by a supreme intelligence for a species that is not quite as intelligent as we sometimes like to believe. There is a lot of room for error in interpretation.

The church today is made up of intelligent, thoughtful members who want to see what the Bible holds for man, but fail to relate the seemingly impossible tales and events described in Genesis to the knowledge that we all now have access to. With the explosion of knowledge, research, and new discoveries this century, it has become harder for the religious community to maintain some of the positions that it has held for centuries, without some degree of compromise. It was a long time before the church accepted the idea that the Earth went around the sun and not vice versa.

It is at this point that an important clarification needs to be made. Some statements that will be proposed later in this book may seem to the reader to advocate a belief in evolution as it is proposed today. That is incorrect. It needs to be made clear what this author means by "Evolution"

In a statement that evolution, or natural selection, played a large part in the development of the primitive or "early man", as described by the science books, **it is not intended to convey that I mean that life on this planet originated by accident.**

Only the concept that nature, through selective breeding, changes all life to be adaptable to the conditions it encounters in order to survive, should be considered. The theories about how organic molecules in a soupy mixture of the early seas of Earth accidentally came together to form cells and DNA strands, are more a product of an overworked modern day imagination than the original Darwinian theory of Evolution. Such statements are based entirely on speculation and guesswork. This is a theory that has never been achieved in the laboratory in any way except to create a few non-living organic chemicals, and is dependent strongly on the laws of probability. Even that argument is weak in mathematical circles.

Unfortunately, congregations are sometimes told from the pulpit that, "If you believe in evolution, you can't believe in God". Ask those pastors if they have read Darwin's "On the Origin of Species", and they most likely will say "no". They are certainly referring to the idea that life began by accident on Earth. This is an idea that they have either read in the newspaper or heard on the media. When a pastor or evangelist makes such a statement, a statement that goes against the facts that every intelligent and informed Christian knows is true and reasonable, it actually discourages the believer from trying to reconcile these differences through a deeper understanding of the passages in the Bible. This creates doubt in the minds of the thinking churchgoers about the truth of the Bible, and prevents them from examining more closely such stories as the ages of the patriarchs, the Flood of Noah, and the Garden of Eden, and encourages them to think that this part of the Bible didn't really happen. We should never be afraid to compare the Bible to facts that we know to be true. It will withstand any test we can apply.

Fifty years ago every thinking person doubted that anyone could live 900 years, but that position has changed dramatically in the last few years with the discoveries now being made in DNA research.

An Associated Press news item that appeared in newspapers worldwide on December 15, 2000, described scientists finding a single gene that could be modified to extend the life of fruit flies by as much as 3 times their normal lifespan. The same improvement in humans would mean that a normal lifespan would be approximately 250 years. There has since been other genes related to longevity discovered. If increasing life spans by any amount is possible simply by altering certain genes, then it is clearly possible that a genetically different "human" could have lived for hundreds of years.

It was predicted during the recent Olympics that by 2008 we would see genetically altered athletes in competition. Perhaps in the near future research will have confirmed that genetic engineering could indeed allow humans to live for hundreds of years, just as the patriarchs did in Genesis.

Scientists and Biologists all accept the concept that without the environmental conditions that are present on Earth, life could not have existed. More and more, we are seeing that the planet Earth is an exception to the norm for heavenly bodies, to the extreme. In fact, nowhere in our solar system have we seen any planet or body that even remotely comes close to having all of the necessities for life, water, oxygen, and hydrocarbon molecules. Because of this, there should be at least some thought and research devoted to finding out *why* the Earth is so special, and the possibility that it may be so by "intelligent design".

There is an attitude of bias and rejection in the average scientist against supporting any hypothesis that might appear to support the Bible. That is regrettable because the Bible still has much information in it that can help to further our understanding of the world of 6000 years ago.

No other document is so detailed in its historical and genealogy content concerning what happened in the Mesopotamian area during that period. Anyone who is really seeking the truth should not allow the past to color his or her attitudes toward the source of truth, regardless of which direction it comes from.

A popular belief being advocated among the "intellectual elite" is that because Babylonian and Sumerian texts predate Moses and also contain stories about the Garden of Eden and the Flood, then the Hebrew Bible must have been derived from those texts while the Jews were in exile in Babylon. It only takes one to read the book of Genesis to see that there is much more detail in the book of Genesis of the Bible than the Babylonian texts. Where did this detail come from? The answer is that the history of man was passed down orally through the direct line of Adam through the descendants of Noah exactly as written in Genesis. The Babylonians knew the story of the flood and the garden because the descendants of Noah were the ones who settled the plains of "Shinar" or Sumer as we now call it. It was these settlers that "founded" the city of Babylon. Why the truth was not written down in ancient Babylon is that the first descendants of Noah were accepted as "Gods" themselves and it was tempting for them to remain silent and not tell the whole story because it would have lessened their stature. If someone treats you as a "God", its tempting to remain silent that there is a greater God that they don't know about.

Can any other culture trace its genealogy directly back to the first human? The Babylonian texts only go back to Noah and make clear the interaction of his descendants with the early humans through stories like "The Epic of Gilgamesh". In this story Gilgamesh, a king in Babylon, makes the incredible statement that he is 2/3 God through marriage. Gilgamesh was a product of a descendant of Noah and another, lesser descendant. This fits exactly the idea that the first pure settlers from the flood were accepted as Gods and married into the inhabitants of that region. As these God-like men took mortal wives, the first offspring would be ½ Gods and the next generation could be said to be ¼ Gods. There are many examples in ancient literature of individuals being ¼, 1/8, and other fractional parts, Gods. These are present in all the great civilizations of the ancient world, such as Egypt, Greece, and Babylon.

Einstein made the comment that "Religion without science is blind, and science without religion is lame". Both claim to be searching for, and have some form of, the truth.

With this in mind, is it possible that the Bible could be absolutely accurate in everything it says and still not conflict with what we know to be true in the "real" world? Can the accounts described in the book of Genesis be reconciled with current known scientific facts? I believe they can if we can separate "facts" from "interpretations", a critical difference that both the religious and the scientific community have failed to discern. Let us now try to put the pieces of the puzzle together.

Chapter Three

THE PLAN DEVELOPS

Genesis 1:27 says that Man was deliberately made in the image of God. That passage doesn't necessarily apply to how we look. Only an entity of infinite intelligence could have conceived of a creating a being with our "weaknesses". It is our complexity of emotions, feelings, and qualities that don't contribute to "survival", that separate us from other creatures that developed through natural selection. Loving and caring for the weak is an emotion that would be foreign and a weakness in the realm of "survival of the fittest". It had to come from someone higher in intelligence.

Because we seldom start something complex without first having a plan, the same must have been true in Genesis 1:1. In fact, the purpose of this book is to attempt to explain how everything that is described in the Bible is part of a coordinated, highly complex plan. The hardest part of writing this book was how to explain some of the core concepts that are necessary in a way that will seem right and acceptable to both traditional believers and serious science readers. This author had great problems with some of the ideas because they went against what had been accepted traditionally from my youth to be true. After finally biting the bullet and playing a game of what if . . . things started happening. The result was that a puzzle, which had previously defied logic, suddenly began falling together into a neat, organized picture of God, His plan, and the history of Man. The picture that was developing was too perfect to ignore.

Realizing that the following statements may offend some people of faith, I ask that, before rejecting them, you consider the arguments presented in the chapters following and look at the complete picture. You may find that it makes more sense than your previous conception of this important story.

Concept number 1: The universe really is 12-15 billion years old.

The book of Daniel in the Old Testament states very clearly that God's years are not our years. God's time is measured differently and a "day" with the Lord" may not be 24 hours as we know it. We have ample evidence that the Earth is older than 6000 years, and we've all heard the arguments against radiocarbon dating. It's not perfect but its not the only way to tell how old something is. The floor of the Atlantic Ocean is spreading by a measurable amount in so many inches each year. Interpolation backward in time tells us that the continents were joined much longer than 6000 years ago. There are features and layers of rock on the east coast of South America that match perfectly the same features on the west coast of Africa. The evidence left by the Ice Ages tells us that it took much longer to create and melt a one-mile thick sheet of ice that covered two thirds of North America than 6000 years.

Radiocarbon dating is the principal method for dating very old artifacts and is often criticized as being inaccurate. It has its limitations and is not perfect, but it can generally be accepted as a means for finding a "ballpark" figure for the age of an object. There are other methods but all have limitations.

Having heard and read all the arguments against these measurements, you have to conclude that when you have to stretch something so many times in so many different ways to make it fit, that maybe the simplest explanation is the best one. That maybe the Earth really is that old. There is the argument that God could have instantly aged everything after creation to look old and my reply is, "Why would he need to". He has all the time in the world and it has always appeared to me that God saves his miracles for only emergencies that cannot be resolved in other, natural ways. God seems to prefer a "natural" solution to a problem over waving His hand and performing a miracle, and given a choice always chooses the former. Too many people of faith prefer a miracle instead of a natural solution. In any case, even if the aging theory were correct it would only be correct for God. From our standpoint the age of the universe would still be older than 6000 years.

It is important that we accept that there was a world long before the Garden of Eden because: 1. Genesis clearly puts the garden in the second chapter, after the seven days of creation, 2. The Bible tells us that the creation of the universe and the Earth took 6 of God's days, days that began even before there was an Earth to rotate every 24 hours, and 3. To understand the plan for the garden and the created man, Adam, there had to be a world already existing outside the garden, fully formed and populated with all kinds of animals, including some semi-intelligent bipedal hominid forms.

Concept Number Two: An early form of man did develop from the forces of evolution, with a little help from God.

Realizing that the anti-evolutionists will strongly object to this next statement, it still has to be said. Evidence supports the idea that development of all life on earth took place over hundreds of millions of years in pretty much the way the scientists have said, *with the exception of how it started.* Many people associate believing in evolution with the belief that life on Earth happened by accident. The first living cell didn't just develop as an accident of chemistry in a muddy pond of water, but was planted by an intelligent being. It was after that happened that God said "Let the Earth bring forth", and natural conditions dictated how different animals developed, just as they do today.

Why propose that the forces of evolution helped to create the millions of species of life on this planet? Because of all the evidence available, and the statement in Genesis 1:11 "And God said, Let the Earth bring forth vegetation, the herb yielding seed after its kind, and the fruit tree yielding fruit after its kind", is a powerful one that suggests when God said "Let", it meant He allowed forces in nature to facilitate the creation of all our different species of plant and animal life. If that is true then there has to be some truth to that part of the theory of evolution. That's not to say that God didn't plant the first seed or cell that all other life came from. Evolution by "Intelligent Design" is a concept that is becoming more accepted in both scientific circles as well as the religious community. Selective breeding can create variations in animals that would never occur otherwise. Our vegetables today taste better than our grandparents' did, not because of genetic engineering, but because of genetic selection of the best plants to produce a better strain of that plant.

To accept that premise is not saying that God didn't create all our varieties of animal and plant life. He created the environment on Earth that would result in an abundance of life and its possible that He may have even intervened from time to time to help it along. The Earth was like a garden. He planted the seed of the first life, nurtured it, and the Earth grew it.

The statement in Genesis 1:26 describes the creation of the early form of Man. God said "Let us make man in our image . . ." This suggests that God took a personal interest in the creation of man and did not allow evolutionary forces to dictate entirely his creation and development. It also suggests to me that the plan for the eventual destiny of man was conceived before The Garden of Eden and Adam. This could have taken place in several ways. God could have taken a creature already existing such as the earliest "scientific version" of man, Australopithecus, and genetically re-engineered him at some point in the dim past, putting him on the road of development to become present day man, or He could have simply created Homo sapiens to be the creature that modern science books describe as "early man". However He did it, my contention is that this form of man was on the earth for thousands of years before Adam or the Garden of Eden was created.

Concept Number Three: After God created the universe billions of years ago, He came back to the Earth 6000 years ago and created the Garden of Eden.

As was discussed earlier in chapter 1, this has to be considered as one of the major breakthroughs that dictated the direction this book would take. It took a while before I realized it, and it came by accident. The two versions of the creation described in Genesis 1 and 2 are really describing two different times that God created life on Earth.

The first one took place in the 6 days of God in which he created the Heavens and the Earth. During these 6 days God said, "Let the Earth bring forth . . ." several times and announced the creation of plant life and animal life on Earth.

This narrative in Genesis, chapter one, describes the entire time span of 12-15 billion years of development in which the sun, the stars, the moon, and the Earth developed according to natural, physical laws from the time that God set those laws in motion. The phrase "Let the Earth." indicates that he allowed physical and natural laws to determine the creation of all the species of plants and animals on the Earth

The second creation event, described in Genesis, chapter two, took place around 6000 years ago and began with God creating the Garden of Eden "in the east of Eden".

The important idea that I want to present here is that after God created this Earth some 5 billion years ago, he chose to come back to it at a much later date to create something else. That "something else" was to result in everything that we have today and would create the technological society we now enjoy or tolerate, depending on your viewpoint. The question now to answer is "What was God doing in the Garden of Eden?"

Concept Number Four: The "World" that was destroyed by God in the flood of Noah was the large, but local, area the Bible calls "Eden".

This is a powerful statement that I struggled with for a long time before committing to it. Two scientists, William b. Ryan and Walter C. Pitman, have presented a very convincing argument in their book *Noah's Flood*, that the Flood event was due to a very deep depression that was carved out by retreating glaciers just after the Ice Age, being suddenly inundated by a catastrophic deluge and creating the present Black Sea. The area, which contains approximately 150,000 square miles and lies 650 feet below the level of the Mediterranean, just 20 miles away, was flooded when a narrow neck of land that held back the Mediterranean Sea, suddenly broke through and allowed the full force of the seas beyond to rush in.

Ryan and Pitman document the research that they have conducted over the past 20 years which proves that a catastrophic flood did occur in the area traditionally accepted as the original location of the Garden of Eden, and the date given of articles recovered from the floor of the sea, under 650 feet of water, by radiocarbon dating, roughly corresponds to the time traditionally held as the time period of the "Genesis" flood. This was an area with a natural boundary, the rim of the depression described earlier. Science is finally catching up and learning the truths that have always been available in the Bible.

After accepting that fundamental argument, so many things fell into place and were explained by it that I could not go back to the universal destruction theory proposed by the fundamentalists.

The statement "All that God created was destroyed" was still a problem and has always been interpreted to mean "since the creation of the world". This trap has promoted and sustained the idea that the whole planet Earth was flooded to the same level. If we re-interpret the statement above to read "All that God had created since creating the Garden of Eden", we can change our planet-wide view of destruction to include only the area immediate to the garden, since none of his 'most recent' creations existed in the rest of the world.

There is another strong reason to believe that the flood destruction event was not worldwide. In the original Hebrew text, the version that is ascribed to being written by God's hand and given to Moses on Sinai, the story uses only two ancient Hebrew words, "Erets" and "Adamah" to describe the extent of the destruction. The common translation of the main word used, "Erets", in English Bibles, is Earth. Its common usage in ancient times was to refer only to land or a country.

We use the word Earth ourselves to refer to the substance we plant crops in, or the use of the ground. If I say that the earth is rich and good for my corn crop, you understand that I'm not referring to "Planet Earth." When we translate the genesis story of the flood that the water covered the "Earth", it would be just as proper to say that the flood "covered the ground", according to the way that the Hebrew people used that word in those times. The other word, "Adamah", used in Genesis to describe the destruction of the flood, is also used to refer to a country or a land area.

To support this argument, there is a reference in Samuel 30:16 to an army of David being spread "abroad over all the Earth". In the original Hebrew Bible the word used for Earth in this case is the same word, "Erets", used earlier to refer to the destruction of Noah's flood. It is obvious from the text that the only area inhabited by the army was the land of the Philistines. Should we apply a "literal translation" to this passage also and say that David's army conquered the whole world? Yet we use that same logic to translate the same Hebrew word used in this text, as used in Genesis chapter 7 to describe the extent of the flood. In Samuel 30:16 it refers only to a land area or a "country". It is likely that the use of the same word in Genesis 7 also refers to only a land area, the area contained within the place God called Eden.

The Bible was written over 3000 years ago and almost nothing was known by the Hebrew people of the civilizations living in other parts of the Earth. God wrote the Bible for those who would read it at that time for understanding, which were the Hebrew people who followed Moses after his encounter with God at Mount Sinai.

The point of these arguments is that there have been many times and many areas that have been called "The World" which were really only local areas. The problem is a semantic one caused by errors in translating terms that have more than one meaning. I believe that the word "world" or "Earth" as used in Genesis, refers only to the part of the world or Earth that was known by the pre-flood descendants of Adam, an area that included everything that was within the boundaries of Eden.

Hopefully, we are beginning to see that whenever the Bible mentions destroying a part of God's creation it is referring only to the areas and things created after He created the Garden of Eden, and not the creation described in Genesis chapter 1. It seems reasonable to assume that God's intent was to destroy all that He had created AFTER Genesis 2.4, after coming back to the Earth sometime around 4000 B.C., and creating the Garden of Eden. If that were true, then the destruction of the "world" would be limited to the area contained within what the Bible calls Eden.

Remember that Eden was the larger area in which only a part of it, "in the East", was set aside for a "Garden", hence the Garden of Eden. When you speak of "Eden" many people think only of the Garden of Eden. As I will explain later the larger area called Eden was in fact a sizable area that included all of today's Black Sea area, which is now under water, and parts of the country of Turkey.

Concept Number Five: All the great civilizations that developed in the Second Millennium B.C. can trace their beginnings, their Gods, and their religions back to "visitors" who were direct descendants of Noah,

who came to their ancestors with great knowledge and abilities, and taught them skills in agriculture, writings, language, and government.

After Noah and his family settled in the mountains of Ararat after the flood, it took only 100 years for their numbers to increase to the point that they could migrate to all the inhabited areas of the Mesopotamia and the Mediterranean. Genesis 11:2 calls the first area of settlement outside of the Ararat landing "the plains of Shinar". Archeology and historical research confirms that this is another word for the land of Shumer, or Sumer, as a mistake in spelling now calls it. All historians accept the Sumerians as the first people to show evidence of modern civilization and government.

When this happened they encountered the primitive descendants of "Early Man" and were immediately received as "superior" beings who were carrying with them the fruits of the creations of God in the Garden of Eden. These included improved seeds and strains of Wheat, Barley, Rye, other vegetables, improved fruit trees for greater nutrition and yield, and certain animal varieties that were saved on the ark.

The inhabitants received them as Gods because they didn't seem to die. If you consider that the lifespan of these descendants of Noah was still several hundred years, when the average lifespan of Homo sapiens at that time was about 35 years, it is not hard to see why they were considered Gods. With the average lifespan of the primitive beings they encountered being less than 40 years, their lifetime would be across several generations with the result that no primitive would ever see one of these individuals be born and die within their own lifetime.

When God told Noah to save all the animals and seeds, he was referring to His creations in the Garden of Eden. Saving samples of these creations and the Adamic form of Man himself was the purpose of the ark.

Concept Number Six: God's reason for the Garden, Adam, and all of the subsequent events, was to eventually bring the existing races of primitive man to a higher level of morality, civilization, and technology, in preparation for the day when certain members of the human race would be accepted into the "Kingdom of God".

It was God's plan from the beginning, after creating the plants, fruit trees, animals, and Adam and Eve in the garden, to disperse these "gifts" to primitive man throughout the world. In Genesis 6:7 when God decided to destroy "Man whom I have created", he is not saying that He was going to destroy the whole human race but ONLY the species of man that was created in the Garden of Eden and his descendants. The words *"Man whom I have created from the face of the Earth*" imply that there is another form of Man that was created differently from the one in the Garden. If there was only one form of man why use the phrase "Man whom I have created from the face of the Earth". If the statement "whom I have created", is referring to the "grand creation of all things" of chapter one, it would be sufficient to just say "man".

Some will argue that "All things were created by God", and they are right. It seems that it was necessary to differentiate between the two "creations" in this statement. This is simply a play of words in the Bible referring specifically to the most recent "creation" event, the one in the Garden. The first form of man was created on the Earth when God said "Let the Earth bring forth . . .", followed by "Let us make man in our image . . .", in chapter one, verse 26. The Garden creation of man involved God Himself making man from the dust, with no assistance from the forces of nature. This explains why the Bible is so specific in using the words "Man whom I have created from the face of the Earth". *Only the man created in the Garden of Eden, the one that was created "from the face of the Earth", is the one God is speaking of destroying.* The Homo sapiens man who was a product of Genesis 1:26, that was living outside that area at that time, was not created in the garden, and was not destroyed.

The plan for "Homo sapiens'" improvement was to be accomplished through the mixing of the genes of descendants of Adam and Noah with the primitive inhabitants of the areas around the original "Eden". It was these "colonies" of visitation that later became the great civilizations of Babylon, Egypt, Greece, Assyria, and others.

It is obvious from God's actions concerning the Flood, the tower of Babel, Abraham, Moses, and the history of the Hebrew people that He intended from the beginning to develop the culture, morals, and abilities of man in slow, concrete steps over the centuries. His plan was to eventually enable man to accept the concept of a time when there would be a separation of mankind into those who were ready for admission into His order, or kingdom, and those who refuse to rise above their primitive origins.

These are the primary concepts that form the basis for the message in this book. All subsequent chapters will deal with supporting facts and arguments, and why I believe these ideas to be accurate and true, and show a much larger story than just the garden or the flood alone.

Chapter Four

THE TWO CREATIONS

Having read and re-read Genesis 1 and 2 many times and spending hours trying to make the events described in these two chapters fit with what I knew to be scientifically accurate, I came to some conclusions. I knew that the narrative of the six days was chronologically accurate with known Science. These are the events as described both by the Bible and by the science books.

The first thing created in both the "Big Bang" theory and the Bible was Light and even science cannot take us back before that event and explain the cause of the initial explosion, except to say that it was a "quantum fluctuation".

We have just as much right to assume that a higher intelligence or "God" created it as science does to say otherwise. We have an explanation and they plainly admit that they don't.

After the creation of light, the order of the other creations follows, almost to the letter, the description in our high school textbooks. The infinitely hot plasma or "light" divided and coalesced into solid objects. This is the point where our science books say that atomic and sub-atomic particles first came into being, and space, instead of being filled with radiation, or the "light", now had areas filled with matter and vacuum as "God divided the waters from the waters."

Its interesting that the "plasma" that the scientists say was the first thing that existed, is treated in computer simulations as a "fluid" and a whole branch of science is devoted to "fluid" Mechanics. We normally think of a fluid as being of the "water" variety. This was the First Day.

"And God said 'Let there be a firmament in the midst of the waters, and let it divide the waters from the waters.'" This was when the atoms through the attraction of gravity came together to create objects with structure, and the galaxies and stars began to form. This is exactly what our textbooks say was the next event in creation. So far there is no disagreement. This was the Second Day.

"And God said 'let the waters under the heaven be gathered together into one place and let the dry land appear'. This describes when the science books say that the planets, comets, and asteroids formed. Notice that the Bible says that the material that they were formed from was "gathered together".

Astronomers say that the planets were formed when the debris that was left over from the formation of a star began to encircle and orbit the star as nothing more than a cloud of small particles, and the solid material in a particular orbit was "scooped up" or gathered together by the new emerging proto-planet. It is a fact that until this happens there is no such thing as "Dry Land". The material that formed the star or sun was white hot and was still in a liquid or molten state and the leftover material was like a kind of "dust" in orbit around it. The "Gathering Together" took place when the first solid body formed in an orbit and began to circle the star. As it moved along in its orbit it swept the orbit clean of excess material, at the same time growing in size from adding new material to its structure. This was how the Earth formed according to science and the Bible. It's interesting that the science books also say that this could have happened even before the central sun was fully formed and began to give off heat and light. The fusion process that causes a star to give off light requires that gravity shrink the body of gases to a size that the central temperature of the star reaches 100 million degrees. The Bible confirms this by creating the Sun and Moon after the Earth formed.

The Bible says "And God called the dry land Earth". At the same time that the Earth was being formed the different materials that made up its structure were collecting together and the water that was present, being lighter than the metals and other materials of the inner Earth, floated on the surface and created the "Seas", or oceans.

The next verse states that the first living things on the Earth were plants, and that is exactly what the science books say. The passage in Genesis 1 where God says, "Let the Earth bring forth . . .". seems to support the hypothesis that life developed according to natural laws and conditions on the Earth. The statement "yielding seed . . . whose seed was in itself", is confirmation that the ability to reproduce itself and produce seed was the first requirement for life to exist, also as reported in the science books. This ended the Third Day.

The next "creation event" was to create the satellite of Earth, the Moon. Even our science books now say that the moon was either created or captured by the Earth at some point after the Earth itself was formed.

It took some time for the first light from the stars to reach Earth because of the vast distances it has to travel. Today when you look up at the night sky, there are many stars that are so far away that the light from them takes millions of years to reach us after it is emitted. Some stars could have existed for millions of years before they were ever seen from the Earth and the emphasis in verse 15 is on the light that they give to the Earth. This ended the Fourth Day.

The first animal life on Earth began in the oceans and moved later onto the land as described in verse 20. Later certain animals developed wings and birds were created. The mammals were among the last animal species to develop and, as told in verses 21-25, whales and cattle are among the last to be created.

Every science book now in print states that Man has existed on Earth for a very short time and verse 26 confirms this because Man is the last to be created. The "man" this is speaking of is the same man that our science books call Australopithecus, or the earliest form of man on Earth. This took place approximately two and a half million years ago according to science.

It is interesting that after all of the "Let . . ." statements in chapter 1, God himself takes a hand in the creation of Man and says "Let us make Man in our image". This statement in the Bible tells me that after evolution had formed all the other life forms of the Earth, God Himself deliberately intervened to change the DNA of an existing creature to form a new line of being that would eventually develop to become early "man", with a little help along the way.

Let me clarify that this "man" it is speaking of is the "Homo sapiens" man that was on the Earth before Adam and coexisted with him for a time. It is also my feeling that the passage is more an announcement of God's plan for man than an action that was immediately executed. He is not 'commanding' man into existence but is announcing the beginning of a process. The making of "Man in our image" was to be a process that was begun in Genesis, chapter one, expanded in Genesis, chapter 2, and continues to this day.

This is not contradictory to science that says that if the history of the Earth were a 12-hour clock, then man would have been in existence only in the eleventh hour and the 59th minute. This ended the Sixth Day. Thus ended the "six days of creation" according to Genesis 1-31.

For centuries, theologians have debated why Genesis includes a second account of the creation, beginning in chapter 2, verse 6. Many concluded that it was simply describing some of the events that happened in Genesis 1 in greater detail, but the order of it seemed to suggest something else.

The puzzle was that both chapters mention the creation of man and gives the impression that they are both describing the same event. The wording which says "and the Lord formed Man . . .", and "And the Lord planted a Garden . . ." reads like it is a continuation of the events that started in Genesis 1. If it was describing the same events as previous verses I wouldn't expect a sentence to begin with "and". It should say something like "At the time that . . .". "And" suggests an event that takes place after something else has happened.

As I was writing this book I remained puzzled by these passages and the "repeating" of certain creation events. After some thought as to why this is, it occurred to me that if God first created the heavens and the Earth, and later came back to Earth around 6000 years ago, and began creating certain things in the "Garden of Eden", separate from the original creation, that maybe the second version of the creation story had to do with only the events that took place at that time.

In other words, there were two separate creation events that needed two creation stories. The two versions of the creation have puzzled Bible scholars for centuries but it becomes clear if we consider that there was a great lapse of time between the original creation and the one 6000 years ago. We really don't know how many times God came to earth to intervene in the development of this planet but it is clear that from Genesis 2:7 on, the events described all occur after he created the Garden of Eden, and that was approximately 6000 years ago.

What finally convinced me that this is describing a separate, different event was when I re-read it and realized that everything that follows in this chapter refers to life that was created in the Garden. The second version is very specific that "out of the ground made the Lord God to grow every tree that is pleasant to the sight, and good for food." After he planted the garden, God was conducting some "genetic engineering", to use a modern term, to improve and create new varieties of plant life for the benefit of "Homo sapiens" the primitive early man that was a product of evolution, that began to develop in chapter 1, verse 27. The use of the term "good for food" indicates his desire to provide a nutritious food source that would be easy to cultivate.

Most of the existing plant sources of food for the primitive man outside the garden were either hard to gather, such as berries, or not very nutritious. The wheat plant that existed then was a wild form of wheat that was not as nutritious as today's variety and produced fewer yields. All men of science that study this period of man's history agree that it was during this epoch of 2600 B. C. to 2900 B. C., that somehow, a refined variety of wheat, that provided more nutrition, and was also more productive, and easier to cultivate, suddenly arrived on the scene without any explanation. The amazing thing associated with this event is that the "new" wheat had quadruple the number of chromosomes that the old wheat did. Certainly, something genetic had taken place outside of evolution to create a new species. Chromosomes don't multiply overnight in the natural world.

That confirmed the realization that the "Garden creation" was a separate event from the "Heavens and Earth" creation time period of Genesis 1-31. If you read Genesis 1:26 and Genesis 2:7 you see man being created on two different occasions. The last time was when he created Adam, who was not exactly the same as the "man" mentioned in the first account. It is Adam, and only Adam's line that the Bible recognizes as being the "true" man.

Frank R. Klassen in 1972 wrote The Chronology of the Bible in which he gives the date of the Garden of Eden creation as 3975 BC. When I looked at the painstaking research he conducted and the meticulous calculations he made on every age and date by cross-referencing, whenever possible, all events in the Bible, I have to believe that his date is probably the most accurate. Most Bible scholars agree to a date sometime around 3600-4000 BC. There is some historical evidence for it being before this but the exact time or period is a subject for speculation.

There is a belief in some circles that there are "gaps" in the genealogy as given in Genesis because of statements in other books of the Bible that list the lines of descent slightly differently. This argument has been used to justify an earlier time for the Garden of Eden, and that argument may be valid. This could possibly account for another 1000 years but many people today believe that man has only been on Earth for 6000 years since the Garden of Eden, and that the last 1000 years, or the 7th day in God's timetable, are about to begin. In the absence of overwhelming evidence of that "gap", I will continue to accept the genealogy as given, to be true and accurate.

Look in any history textbook on the development of man and it will invariably begin with "early man" who lived about 100,000 years ago or earlier. We look around today and see man as an intelligent creature that is capable of traveling to the moon or solving the genetic code of the human race. With all the different designations for "man" such as Homo Erectus, Cro-Magnum, or Neanderthal man, we can easily get the impression that the term "man" applies to any upright, bipedal hominid that can make tools and communicate

Chapter Five

THE GARDEN, THE RIGHT PLACE AT THE RIGHT TIME.

The story of modern Man does in fact begin in the Garden of Eden. A question that must be asked and answered is, "Why did God choose this time and place to plan the birth of civilized mankind?" The answer lies in the fact that several factors affecting man's development, came to be optimum at the same time. The most important factor was the climate.

For the previous 20,000 years the whole Earth had been under a blanket of glacial ice, engulfed in one of many similar ice ages that had become regular and common in the last 1,000,000 years. Some scientists believe the cause of the climatic cycle was somehow due to the precession of the North Pole, which completes a circle every 26,000 years. Whatever the cause, the Earth began to change to a warmer, more humid climate around 11,000 years ago. By 6,000 years ago most of the glaciers had retreated beyond the Arctic Circle and the atmosphere increased in temperature and humidity, and allowed for plentiful rainfall over areas that had previously received very little rain.

This was an important development for Man because serious agriculture was not possible or productive enough to sustain entirely a primitive culture, as it had existed before that change in the weather. The conditions were right for Man to become a farmer, if he only had the necessary knowledge and the right crops.

It was just after this period that suddenly Man discovered a myriad of new plants that did not require a great deal of care to be very fruitful and productive. These included the previously mentioned new strain of wheat that did not exist before 3,000 B. C., fruit trees that could be harvested and cultivated, certain vegetables that man suddenly discovered that were nutritious and relatively easy to grow, and grapes.

It is in the book of Genesis that the grape was first mentioned in history when it describes Noah as the first wine maker and a tender of vineyards. The history books also credit the area in Armenia where the Bible says that Noah landed the Ark, as having the first records of grapes being harvested for food.

This period also saw Man domesticating certain animals and their products for food, clothing, and shelter, for the first time. Sheep, goats, cattle, and other common farm animals began to be a large part of man's culture. These developments could not have happened before the end of the ice age.

The time was also right for man to make a quantum leap in his physical development. The previous 1,000,000 years had seen primitive man leave all other animals behind in intelligence. No other animal had come close to the art of tool making or the beginnings of a language that Man had achieved. Though it was still a primitive art, the ability to make a stone ax or hammer, and use animal bone and thread to sew together clothing was something no other creature could begin to achieve. It took very little genetic manipulation to bring that form of Man to the creature that we call modern man today.

The place God chose for the birth of civilization was unique also. The fertile crescent is described in all science books as being the cradle of civilization, because it was an area that provided everything man needed in order to develop an advanced civilization. The ground was rich in the area between the Tigris and the Euphrates rivers and provided water for irrigation and soil for agriculture. Abundant clay was also available to make the bricks that were needed for large buildings and cities. The climate was right for a long productive growing season. The dryness of the area also helped preserve knowledge through written works and scrolls. It was surrounded by waterways for travel and navigation to other parts of the world. Timber was plentiful for construction of furniture, ships, and tools. Man had gone from straw huts with earthen beds to brick homes with wooden furniture in little more than 2000 years. Of all places in the world, this area probably had more of the necessary ingredients for civilization than any other.

All of these things contributed to the period of 6,000 years ago being the right time for God to choose to bring Man forward to the age we now live in, an age of culture, arts, science, technology, civilization, and understanding.

The remarkable thing that I fail to understand is how so many intelligent products of this event can insist that all of the events that I have just described, events that happened in such a short geologic period, were accidental. If it were an accident, it is an accident that didn't happen in the previous two million years of human history on this planet. I can only conclude that it happened by design, the design that the book of Genesis calls the Garden of Eden.

The Bible says that it was located in the eastern part of a larger area called Eden. The earliest civilization ever recorded was that of the Sumerians who left a clay tablet library that numbered over 25,000 documents buried in the sands of Mesopotamia, with their own version of the Genesis story imprinted in them. These were only discovered in 1876 by an English archeologist named George Smith, who was astonished to find texts referring to a "deluge" in ancient artifacts uncovered by the British Museum in London. Diggings in the Mesopotamia area had just uncovered ruins of the cities of Sumer, Assyria, and Nineveh, cities that were considered before that time to be only myths from the Bible.

On one of these tablets was recorded the name E.DEN as the place where the creation began. These tablets would prove to yield much information about the ancient world at the earliest evidence of civilization ever recorded. However, the greatest source of information about what was going on in that area is still the account recorded in Genesis.

Many historians use these tablets and the fact that the Sumerian account of the flood predates the Bible as proof that the Bible was copied from them. The argument is that the book of Genesis was only written around 1300 B.C. and the Sumerian texts were written around 2400 B.C. The Sumerian texts say nothing about Adam and his genealogy, though they do mention a flood and a character similar to Noah. Historians ignore the tradition of oral history that preserved the Genesis account from the beginning as a legitimate record. If the Genesis account came from an earlier Sumerian text then where is the story of Adam, the fall of man, Cain, and the other stories of Genesis?

The Genesis account contains information of a continuous line of descendents, their ages, and much more detail of the creation and the events following the Garden of Eden, which proves that it is the earlier version and that the Sumerian texts are simply a collection of stories preserved on clay tablets by various individuals who knew parts of the story but not the whole story.

Chapter Six

THE NEW MAN

When the Bible talks about "Man" is it talking about the same creature that we just discussed? Lets look and see if they compare.

The first "man" in the Garden of Eden was Adam. Adam at first didn't know the difference between good and evil until his eyes were opened by eating of the tree of knowledge of good and evil, according to Genesis 2:17. He didn't have any children until he was over a hundred years old. He eventually lived for nine hundred and thirty years, and had the ability to talk directly to God. He must have been immune to all diseases that now afflict us or he couldn't have lived 930 years without contracting at least one form of deadly disease. According to passages from *"Legends of the Bible"* by Louis Ginzberg, Adam's body did not decay when he died and had a protective covering on it before the fall. Does this describe anyone you know today?

The point is this, that the first biblical "Man", Adam, was not the same man that the science books describe who lived much earlier on the Earth. In fact it is my contention that the Homo sapiens man was already here on Earth and lived in great numbers in many parts of the world at the time of the "Garden".

It should be emphasized that today's man is also called Homo sapiens, but if my hypothesis is correct, today's version of Homo sapiens is not really the same as he was 6000 years ago. In fact the creature we call Homo sapiens today is not the same creature as either of the two species of man earlier described as living 6000 years ago. Through the intermixing of the two versions of "man" over the past 6000 years, we have today a species of man that is different from either of those previously mentioned. I believe that the genes that were injected into the gene pool of the man existing then by the descendants of Adam and Noah, have had a marked improvement on the species by:

1. Increasing the lifespan from about 40 years to a maximum of 120 years.
2. Causing an increase in his intelligence level in all areas
3. Enhancing the immune system of Man to make him less vulnerable to the diseases that elevated the mortality rate of earlier man.
4. Leaving a residual trace of a sixth sense that enabled Adam and his descendants to communicate with God directly.

It is clear from the passages of Genesis that before the flood God communicated more frequently with man than after. The privilege of communicating with God may have been related to a physical attribute that Adam passed on to later generations. It is the presence of this latter item that I want to discuss in some depth.

The weakness and loss of this latter ability in the "new" species of man after Noah and his sons, may have made it necessary for man to communicate with God through Priests instead of directly, the way Noah, Shem and earlier descendants of Adam did.

After the Flood, Noah's son Shem became the patriarch for all true followers of the God who created Adam. This was because he was the oldest living being on Earth and was the last person to have seen the world before the flood. He still had the ability to communicate with God directly, as Adam did, and as a result was considered a Priest by all men who by that time could not talk to God except through him.

The special communication abilities of Adam had been diminished beyond being useful for man. Shem's name was changed to Melchizidec when he assumed the role of history's first Priest. It's possible that this ability to communicate directly with a higher intelligence may have been a genetic ability that was passed on to descendants of Adam. Recent scientific discoveries support this concept through Mitochondria DNA analysis.

It has been shown by very recent research that everyone who is a descendant of Aaron, the brother of Moses and the first of the line of the Levitical priesthood that was ordained by God, has a specific tracer gene, that is unique to these people.

I would like to quote an excerpt from an article that appeared in the *U.S. News and World Report* magazine in the January 29, 2001 issue, in a report on the rapid use of DNA tracking to find our genetic roots.

> "Andy Carvin is a pioneer on the strange frontier of DNA genealogy. . . . He read about research tracing the Y sex chromosome, which is passed intact from father to son, all the way back to the time of Aaron, the single progenitor of the priestly *COHEN* caste 3000 years ago. More than once, his

father had told him their family was *Cohanim*. 'I was really curious,' Carvin says, 'to see if there was even a small possibility that the oral tradition was true." . . . "Not only did his Y-chromosomes have the *Cohanim* markers-small genetic variations-but other markers matched with those of another man in the database . . . By comparing the variations (Michael) Hammer determined that the Cohanim had a common male ancestor 84 to 130 generations ago—which is around the time of the exodus from Egypt and the original Cohen, Aaron."

This confirms that genetic markers do exist and that the priestly line of Aaron did have specific genes that differentiated their line from others. The fact that we can identify and trace a single gene back to a person who lived 3000 years ago is almost frightening in its implications. We have arrived at a point in our research where genetic identification of this sort is commonplace. Is genetic manipulation of the order that took place in the Garden of Eden too far behind. Will we soon have a "Tree of Life" of our own?

It seems likely that after Noah's descendants were assimilated into the population of man after the flood, this ability to communicate with God was diluted and diminished. This author suggests that it reappeared in a useful but weak form in certain individuals throughout the Old Testament, resulting in those individuals being revered as prophets. It's possible that even today there are rare cases of persons having some form of this weak power.

Catholics have always believed that communications with the Saints through prayer is a legitimate way to get their prayers answered.

Today's Homo sapiens is smarter, more creative, more literate, more analytical, and has a sense of good and evil that was not present in "early man".

The scientists will argue that the genes of one man could not have had much affect on the gene pool of the human race at that time, but there were other factors that came into play. I will show later how Adam's genes did indeed have a large effect on the genetic makeup of modern man.

The time 6000 years ago was a critical period in man's development and was the ideal time for the great leap forward that God had planned for him. Neolithic Man had just learned to use certain tools and there is evidence that he even used fire to make pottery and work with metallurgy to a limited degree. Productive agriculture was barely within his ability but the nutritious crops we know today were not yet available. The wild wheat that was being harvested was hard to grow and was not very nutritious.

It was just a short time later that suddenly and very mysteriously, a more modern form of wheat that somehow had doubled, trebled, then quadrupled their chromosome pairs, appeared on the scene, a genetic mutation of unheard of proportions, in such a short span of time. This new variety of wheat was much more nutritious and easier to cultivate. Instead of one crop per year, it yielded three crops.

Historians have given much credit for man's early rise to civilization, to the ability to grow and cultivate this new variety of wheat. This one development allowed man to enjoy a new standard of living that had never before been seen on this planet. Historians cannot state where it came from except to say that it did not exist 2000 years earlier and it had been unchanged for millions of years before then.

This primitive form of man was not without the capacity to use tools and construct dwellings. He was definitely far above any other form of life in intelligence. His intelligence had been slowly increasing during the past 50,000 years due to the various Ice Ages he had gone through. Each time the world was covered with ice, those who were not resourceful and intelligent enough to cope with the changing conditions did not survive. Darwin's theory of evolution says that as the fittest survive, in time, the whole species will change to be more like those who are better able to adapt. Those who were resourceful and intelligent enough to use fire and animal skins for greater warmth and protection from the cold lived and passed on their genes to guarantee that the next generation also had their intelligence to do the same, and more.

As this happened several times, the intelligence of Homo sapiens was increased gradually with each event to bring him up from the level of other animals, to the point of tool making and language, but the arts of writing and metallurgy were not yet fully developed. The cold forced man to live in groups where a small amount of energy and food could be used more efficiently. This grouping of the species and some sort of social organization necessitated the development of a form of language.

The last Ice Age ended about 11,000 years ago and the water trapped in huge glaciers and ice sheets all over the world began to melt and fill the oceans and lakes. Wherever an ice sheet retreated and left a depression in the Earth, a lake was formed. Such a depression was formed just north of the Mediterranean that resulted in a huge basin where the Black Sea exists today.

About 8000 years ago, because of environmental factors that carried the melting waters north and west, the area of this depression was a desert, except for the shoreline around a small central fresh water lake. The area around the central part of this basin was about 650 feet below the level of the Mediterranean Sea, just a few miles south of the rim. All that prevented the Mediterranean from rushing in and flooding this deep area was a thin span of land only 25 miles wide called the Bosporus Strait. This natural earthen dam held back the force of the oceans beyond. This area would be breached with cataclysmic results later.

The creature that our science textbooks call Homo sapiens man was on the increase in population but still was just a wanderer making a living existing on hunting and gathering food wherever he found it. He lived in nomadic tribes that were small and not very organized. His tools consisted of rock implements. Metal tools that required advanced knowledge of using fire for smelting didn't exist. There was little agriculture and the average lifespan was around 35 to 40 years.

This is the description of man that prevailed at the beginning of the 4th millennium BC, with hardly any variation. There were varieties of this man in many parts of the world. The different races were all present in some form and the differences were pretty much the same as today. There was nothing to stimulate genetic change, which is usually the propagating agent when some evolutionary change takes place. The science textbooks tell us that for a species to undergo a significant change a group must first be isolated from the main body of the species and there must be a drastic environmental force that requires the species to undergo a change in order to survive.

The climate after 10,000 BC remained fairly stable with only minor variations over that time, with little change that could trigger a major shift in the way the humans lived. Yet something did cause a change in the species of "man" and his way of living and thinking that resulted in man drastically re-inventing himself almost overnight.

Chapter Seven

EDEN, THE PLACE OF THE FLOOD

Eden And The Area Of The Flood

As was explained earlier, the word translated as "the whole Earth" or "the World" in Genesis 7 concerning the extent of the destruction of the flood, was the Hebrew word "Erets", which really means "the ground" or "a large area of ground". The description of the "World" or "Earth" in these passages should have been interpreted to describe only the large area around the huge basin that later became the Black Sea.

If we accept that this text is describing a smaller area than the WHOLE Earth, then the statement in Genesis 2:5 makes more sense.

The meaning of the text should be interpreted that in that particular area the ground (earth) was dry because there had been no rain. This matches perfectly the environment of that area just after the glaciers of the ice age had retreated, around 6000 to 7000 years ago. There is overwhelming evidence of weather and rain over other parts of the Earth before 6000 BC.

The weather was actually very dry in this specific area, southern Europe, because so much water was still trapped in the form of ice in glaciers and the polar caps. In this immediate area the weather had created a unique environment. The 200 mile wide basin was a desert except for a small, freshwater lake in its center. Around the shores of this lake was vegetation which thrived on the fresh water and rich soil.

Genesis 2:5 says that it had not yet rained on the Earth. If this area was truly a dry climate with no rain, it would explain how the basin we now call the Black Sea remained dry except for a small lake in its center. It would seem that some cataclysmic event changed both the terrain and the climate after the flood because Genesis tells us that the first rainbow ever seen by man was seen by Noah and his family after they left the ark. The climate of the area had changed and there was now enough humidity in the air for a rainbow to form.

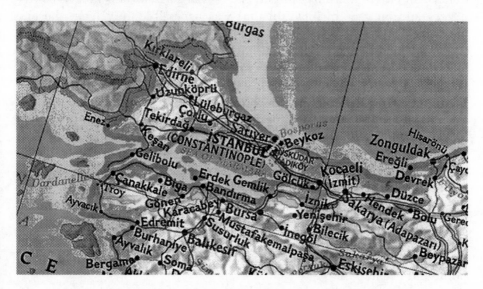

The Bosporus Strait Area

I believe that the area that the Bible calls Eden is actually the area I just described which is now called the Black Sea, and is presently under 650 feet of water. This basin was separated from the Mediterranean by only a narrow neck of land called the Bosporus Strait, which acted as a kind of earthen dam, holding back the vast oceans beyond, only 25 miles away. It also included the mountains of Eastern Turkey, which are southeast of this area.

William Ryan and Walter Pitmen have conducted much research into the natural disaster that covered this area with water, and are convinced that the flood of Noah was actually this disaster. Their recent book *"Noah's Flood"* describes the events that caused the dam to "break" several thousand years ago, resulting in a deluge that flooded the entire area now known as the Black Sea. Ryan and Pitmen estimated that at the Bosporus point where the seas rushed in, almost overnight, the water came in with a force equal to 200 Niagara Falls.

The Bible clearly indicates that the location of the Garden of Eden was in the area of the headwaters of the Tigris and Euphrates rivers. This area is easily identified in the highlands of modern day Turkey, about 50 miles Southeast of the Black Sea shores. Why has no one found evidence of its existence? According to Genesis 3:24 God placed a cherubim at the eastern entrance to the garden to keep Adam and anyone else out.

Why would only one guardian be sufficient to protect the garden? I believe that there was only one entrance to the garden. This would require a very special type of location that was accessible only from the one entrance.

The Epic of Gilgamesh is a Sumerian tale that was recorded on the clay tablets that were found in the remains of the oldest civilization on record. They describe a journey by the fifth king of Sumer to find out if being 2/3 a God is enough to allow him the longevity of the "Gods".

This story describes Gilgamesh finding such a place that he described as "The enclosure of the Gods". The word "enclosure" may be significant in trying to understand the nature of the "Garden".

Gilgamesh arrived at the "Enclosure of the Gods" only after walking many hours through a region that he describes as being very dark. According to the texts," He could see nothing ahead or behind". Finally he broke out into an area of great light, which he describes, as "beautiful as a garden of precious jewels". He begins a description of a "Tree of Life" that he found within the garden, but the tablets are mutilated at this point and are impossible to read.

I would suggest that the area that he passed through that was dark, was a cave, possibly in the mountains of eastern Turkey, that has since been hidden by a landslide through the many years of earthquakes that have taken place in that area. Only a cave would have only one entrance that could be protected by the Cherubim. We don't know what the form of the cherubim was, or the "flaming sword" that it carried, but there are accounts in the same text of an encounter with it by Gilgamesh and his companion, and describes it as a huge creature that could throw a flaming "ray of light" that could kill.

Is it possible that such a place still exists but is hidden from view in such a way that modern man would never find it?

Chapter Eight

THE TREE OF LIFE

Almost all historians agree that the refining and domestication of the wheat crop by the Sumerians around 2200 to 2400 BC was the major contribution to man becoming a farmer and changing from a nomadic existence to one of staying put in an area long enough to build villages and cities. The collective planting and harvesting of the wheat crop required a form of organization and cooperation from the inhabitants that had never been exhibited by man before. Because of the improvement in the standard of living provided by a farming lifestyle, he now had some "free" time on his hands to explore other skills and endeavors that had never been possible before.

However wheat was not the only crop that was refined and domesticated during this time. The cultivation of corn, fruit trees, and management of certain animals was also developed in this very small time period. All of these things dramatically changed man from a mobile, struggling, subsistence way of life to one of a sedentary, urban, civilized one.

This was no small step considering that man, according to the science books had spent the previous 1.5 million years learning how to make and use a stone hammer. The refinement and smelting of metals was another major development that "just happened" to come along at this time. How did man get so "smart" so fast is the intriguing question?

Homo sapiens needed more than just leadership and intelligence to succeed in the world before 4000 BC. Life for mortal man was hard with very primitive agriculture, and little use of tools and metals. Even with tools and knowledge of agriculture, it is my belief that there were not the plants or crops to cultivate that would allow man to succeed sufficiently for him to have time to develop an advanced civilization. It would require constantly working during the daylight hours to provide enough food necessary to sustain life. There were certain refinements and advancements necessary in the genetic makeup of the "crops" available at that time that would have to take place before civilization and agriculture would have a chance to succeed. This is the other part of the "plan" of the Garden.

When God created Adam, his duties were to catalog and record the names of all the creations, both plant and animal in a way that a botanist names and catalogs a new variety of a hybrid species. This was one of Adam's jobs in the garden because it would be Adam's descendants that would later migrate to all parts of the Earth to deliver these "gifts" from God to the Homo sapiens man that was struggling to survive.

Even scientists will universally agree that with gifts like these, man's ability to live a better lifestyle would be greatly enhanced. This would explain where the "refined" wheat seed came from that enabled agriculture to flourish. With other "gifts" such as certain fruit trees that were good to eat, and perhaps even genetically improved or created animals for domestication and growing for food, it is not surprising that primitive tribes of Homo sapiens man might look on someone who brought these gifts to them, as Gods who were bringing to them gifts from heaven. Add to these "gifts" their knowledge of writing, agriculture, metallurgy, and the fact that they were living three and four times the lifespan of the other inhabitants and it is easy to see how they would be revered as "Gods".

The most mysterious part of the story of the Garden of Eden is the part concerning the two trees in the center of the garden. They were called the "Tree of Knowledge of Good and Evil" and the "Tree of Life". Adam and Eve were forbidden to eat of either of these trees. Though Genesis doesn't say anything about God instructing them to not eat of the Tree of Life, it is clear after their sin that the Tree of Life was forbidden to them because the reason they were expelled from the garden was the danger that they would take of it. According to Genesis 3:22, *"And the Lord God said 'Behold, the man is become as one of us, to know good and evil: and now, lest he put forth his hand and take also of the tree of life, and live forever': Therefore the Lord God sent him forth from the garden of Eden, "to till the ground from whence he was taken".*

The question I want to propose here is, were these trees in the normal sense that we think of trees or objects that look like trees to us, such as a "family tree" diagram, or some other object that had branches that made it look like a tree to Adam? In the Epic of Gilgamesh, the hero who finally finds the "Garden of the Gods", says that the trees in the garden looked as if they had precious jewels hanging from them, or on them, which were beautiful to look at.

What would be the reaction of someone from a primitive Mesopotamian village to walking into one of our modern computing centers with all its lights and indicators flashing? The tall equipment racks would appear to be tree trunks to someone who had no previous experience with metal objects and the flashing lights would appear to be berry-like fruits on a tree, that would have the appearance of multicolored jewels.

Today, any such computer that stores information could be called a "Tree of Knowledge". Just as an example of how this could pertain to what was in the Garden, perhaps the Tree of Knowledge of Good and Evil was a storage unit that contained a history of the universe which would also be a history of successes and failures, with successes being "good" and failures being "evil".

Another possibility is that the Tree of Knowledge of Good and Evil could have been something that contained all the "Laws" of God that could not be broken. A modern copy of the Constitution of the United States could be said to be a "book of knowledge of good and evil" since by reading it the reader would know what was "good" or allowed and that which was not.

Obviously, it was not meant for Adam to have access to that knowledge at that time. Too much information could be harmful in the wrong hands. Just as today when a person arrives at an age that he should understand the law, from that time on he is held responsible for keeping it. Until Adam and Eve "knew" good from evil they were not held responsible by God. After they did what they were forbidden to do, they, and everyone who followed them, were held responsible for knowing good from evil.

While we're speculating, and that is all we are doing at this time because we cannot know for sure what was in the Garden, let us consider some possible explanations for what the Tree of Life could have been.

One of the biggest news stories in the science world to become public recently was the story that the human Genome, the genetic code for the human race, has been deciphered. Most scientists expect that at some point soon in our research we will be able to clone a man and perhaps genetically engineer a superior type of human being. It was even announced during the recent Olympics by sportscasters, that by the 2008 Olympics we could look for genetically improved athletes. A recent special program on TV exhibited a device in laboratories today that can routinely break DNA strands to insert certain genes that will alter characteristics of laboratory mice. The lab technicians perform this feat from the keyboard of a computer. The device itself is a separate cabinet with multicolored lights that flash on and off. How hard is it to picture God doing this in the garden if we are almost able to do it now?

What would be the value to science if we had a device that could create DNA artificially, with any structure we programmed into it? If we knew the genetic code for all the animals and plants we know of, could we not create any type of living species we wanted?

Perhaps the Tree of Life was just such a device with the ability to create any form of life artificially by generating the DNA for that species, which could then be used to clone that life form. This would fit in with the other activities taking place in the Garden involving the creation of other life forms. Perhaps the "Tree of Life" was the tool used to perform these miracles. By learning to use this tool, Adam and Eve could have given themselves a body that would never die, giving meaning to the phrase in Genesis 3:22.

With no previous experience with metal objects or anything that could not be seen in nature, a primitive man would most likely describe any such device as a "Tree of Life".

Chapter Nine

WHAT WENT WRONG?

The Bible says that Adam and Eve sinned by defying God's order not to eat of the fruit of the Tree of Knowledge of Good and Evil. Because they were created genetically in the Garden of Eden, they had no knowledge of anything outside the garden. They were created mature adults who were told that their purpose was to tend the garden and to "dress it and keep it". With limited knowledge except for their functions, they were like children who go to school at 5 years old because they are told to, but were too immature to understand why. If the Tree of Knowledge of Good and Evil was a storage facility of a historical nature then accessing it would have immediately educated them to what exists in the outside world, and all the knowledge they needed to understand that the Tree of Life would give them the ability to live forever. The Bible in Genesis says "and the eyes of them were opened" and suddenly they knew.

One of the hardest passages for me to understand was the passage describing Adam and Eve as realizing that they were naked after eating the forbidden fruit. It is easy to understand why that would be a problem in today's society, but why would it be a concern at that time for them. Why would that be so significant to them that they had to hide from God because of it.

The most logical reason is that they realized that something had changed in them from the way they were before they "sinned". They knew immediately that God would see that they had eaten of the tree because of their changed appearance. Why else would they have to hide from God? What would He see that was different from before? Is it possible that they had a "covering" that protected their bodies before eating of the "fruit"?

In the book *"Legends of the Bible"*, by Louis Ginzberg, an oral tradition concerning this story in the garden is described as follows:

"The first result was that Adam and Eve became naked. Before, their bodies had been overlaid with a horny skin, and enveloped with the cloud of glory." After their transgression these "coverings" dropped off and they suddenly saw themselves as "naked".

This is a tale that was handed down outside the official inspired scripture of the Jews.

A television science program on genetic aging that I recently watched suggested that aging is actually caused by damage to the ends of our DNA strands due to random cosmic rays that are invisible to us, but are always bombarding our bodies. I wondered if by shielding ourselves with some lining that would filter out the cosmic rays, we would be able to prevent the DNA damage, thus retarding aging. Perhaps the covering that Adam and Eve had, before their sin caused them to lose it, prevented them from aging. After shedding this "skin" and becoming naked they were fully exposed to the harmful cosmic rays and their aging process immediately began, as foretold by God.

When God warned Adam that he would die the day he ate of the forbidden tree he may have been describing the loss of the protective layer of clothing he had, that prevented his aging process. The "Glorified Cloud" statement reminds us of a passage in the New Testament concerning the rapture, that describes a "Glorified" body that all persons taken would receive, that wouldn't age.

Also interesting is the statement that "In the day you eat of the fruit you will surely die". When we consider that one of God's days is described later in the Bible, as 1000 of our years, the 930 years that Adam lived was an accurate prediction.

The strange passage in Genesis 3:22 concerning God speaking and saying "Let us . . ." indicates that God is talking to someone else present in either the Garden or Heaven. Most likely it was a member of the group of beings called the "Sons of God" who were created before man and had eternal life. In any case, there is the fear that Adam will now know the importance of the Tree of Life and will use it to give himself back the eternal life that he lost by sinning.

It seems that eternal life is a quality reserved only for a select few who are members of God's Kingdom. It's likely that this is the role that all of the "genetically pure" descendants of Adam were to play before the sin in the Garden set man on a different course. The Sons of God as described in both the old and New Testament apparently had that quality and according to the gospel of John, man would eventually regain that quality through the Messiah.

The term "Sons of God", apparently, is a description reserved for those beings that have risen to become worthy of eternal life with God. They were created before man and are probably what many cultures refer to as "Angels". They have the ability to travel from the "Heavenly Abode", and come to the Earth as physical beings. They never die and hold a special place in God's Kingdom that allows them to communicate with Him as they desire. The Bible says that Man was created a little less than the angles. Adam once had the ability to communicate directly with God but lost it, as well as the ability to live without aging, when he sinned in the Garden.

I believe that it is to this kind of state that God wants all men to aspire to and return. The whole purpose of the Garden of Eden was to create those things that would help all mankind to make the jump to an advanced level of civilization so that he may have the chance to become members of this order.

It is appropriate that John 1:12 says "But as many as received Him, to them gave He power to become the sons of God". Becoming worthy is given in the New Testament as accepting Jesus as your advocate to God and becoming like him. Accepting Him and emulating Him are two traits that indicate that a man or woman had reached a level of morality and understanding that justify entering the Kingdom.

There is an event predicted in Thessalonians 4:16 in which those humans who are considered worthy will be taken out of the Earth and transformed with a new "glorified body". It is likely that it is at this time that God will make the final transformation of His Homo sapiens man into a being that can be referred to as a "Son of God". This makes it clear that only "Sons of God" are eligible for entry into God's kingdom. The only way a man or woman can qualify is to be "transformed" into a new being. What will happen to everyone else? The Bible describes God as "Pruning the vineyard" and all those who don't make the journey to the "Heavenly Abode", will be pruned from the branch as well, perhaps doomed to spend eternity "outside the system".

With that in mind it becomes clear what God's plan for man is. He wants man to be changed through a series of steps or improvements to become a new creature that will eventually become a citizen of the Kingdom of God.

Adam's disobedience in the Garden indicates that even a superior race of man is not worthy of that honor. It also becomes evident in Genesis 6 that it is possible for even a group of the elite "Sons of God" to be lacking morally in God's eye and to commit acts in defiance of His will.

Chapter Ten

THE PLAN CORRUPTED

Genesis 6:2 begins with one of the most enigmatic sections of the Bible. It states, "the Sons of God saw the daughters of men that they were fair; and they took them wives of all which they chose." In the next verse God states that Man's years were to be one hundred and twenty years. This is a strange statement, for God had just created Adam whose years were to be nine hundred and thirty years.

All of Adam's descendants before the flood lived at least nine hundred years except for Enoch, who left the Earth to "walk with God". For God to declare that man's years would be one hundred and twenty years indicates that his future plan for mankind would be that his maximum lifespan would be one hundred and twenty years.

At that time the lifespan of the primitive man outside the Garden, was only about 35 to 40 years. I interpret the above passage as God's announced intention for the offspring of Adam to intermix with this primitive man, with the resulting generations to be a race who would be superior to the existing "Homo sapiens" but something less than Adam.

Apparently the offspring of the unions of the "Sons of God" and the daughters of men were a corruption of that plan. Genesis 6:12 says, "And God looked upon the Earth, and behold, it was corrupt; for all flesh had corrupted *His Way* upon the Earth." The important emphasis in this statement is the phrase "had corrupted *His Way* upon the Earth". This indicates that it was not God's *way* for this to happen. God's way was His plan as begun in the Garden of Eden which was supposed to culminate in the lifting of man out of the stone age to the age of civilization. Because of the actions of the "sons of God", this plan was now in chaos.

We have to remember that the inhabitants of the world of "Eden" as told in Genesis chapter 5 were of two kinds, the descendants of Adam and the offspring of the unions between the "Sons of God and the daughters of men".

There may have been some primitive inhabitants in the area of Eden at this time, though they would have been few in number.

The only habitable area would have been the shore of the inner lake of the Black Sea Basin. When Adam was cast out of the Garden he would have probably settled close by out of fear of the outside world that he knew nothing about. His sons and daughters would have found any of these inhabitants and had offspring by them.

It is these offspring that the Sons of God came to Earth and found "Fair" and took as wives. Because of the availability of these "other" genetic sources, it becomes clear why the pure line of Noah was so special, and was described as "perfect in his generation". It didn't take long before there were very few "pure" descendants of Adam left on the Earth.

If Adam was a special kind of "Man" that God created, consider what could have been accomplished by the offspring of the unions between Adam's descendants and the "Sons of God" over the next 1000 years if they had been allowed to remain. Their enhanced abilities would have made them seem as Gods to the rest of the world and would have enabled them to quickly assume control of the whole world.

There is such a civilization described in the writings of Plato. They were described as advanced far beyond any other people on Earth and were "mighty" in power. Genesis 6:4 describes the descendants of the Sons of God and the daughters of men as giants who were also "mighty". Could Genesis 6:1-4 and Plato be describing the same race of people who were mighty, advanced, and were violent. Plato had a name for this race and the place they inhabited. Atlantis. According to Plato, they were also destroyed by a flood in roughly the same time period as described by the Genesis flood.

The term "Sons of God" is a term referring to special beings that apparently came down from the "abode" above the Earth, according to the meaning of the ancient word used to describe them. We can only guess that they were powerful beings that were in existence before man, who inhabited the whole universe, and some of them at least, defied God's wishes by intermixing with his creations on the Earth during this time period.

A point that has not been mentioned in previous discussions about this incident is that it is well known that for any two species to mate and have offspring there must be a great deal of similarity in their DNA. For this to happen there must have been very little difference between Adam's descendents and the "Sons of God". The fact that their offspring in turn had other offspring says a lot about this similarity. In cases such as between the horse and a donkey, two different but similar species, the offspring is sterile and can have no other offspring. Perhaps the inhabitants of heaven are not greatly different from the original Adam. The Bible says that man was created "a little less than the angels". Certainly man has changed somewhat since the flood due to the genetic mixing of Noah's descendents and the primitive man already on the earth, which resulted in "modern man".

The book of Revelation describes a war in the heavens in which one third of the "Angels of God" were cast out of Heaven. A search of historical documents reveals no source for this bit of information other than the mention in the New Testament and in the book of Job. Many books have been written about the "fallen" angels and some suggest that the war itself was over God's creation of Man and his role on the Earth. The Sons of God mentioned in Genesis 6:2 may have been some of the fallen angels who defied God. The Bible describes their offspring as mighty beings who had powers above those of mortal man. There are many references to giants in other passages that suggest that they were not very intelligent.

The word we use today to refer to unintelligible talk is "Gibberish". This word is derived from the ancient word Giboahan, which is another name for the race of giants. Is it possible that the jealousy that the Sons of God had for Man, even with all the powers they possessed, was that God had made man slightly more intelligent than them? After all, rebelling against God was not a mark of high intelligence on the part of Satan. The Bible says of man that he was made "slightly lower than the angels". This could refer to man's size since the offspring of the Angels and primitive man was a race of giants. It could be that the Adamic man, lacking the physical and other attributes that we can only guess at, that the angels had, was actually created as an intelligent being that was superior, at least in Adam's example. If that is true then, as intelligent as we consider ourselves today, by having mixed those genes with the genes of "Homo sapiens", our intelligence prowess, of which we are so proud, is a mere shadow of that of the "First Man".

The strange passage in Genesis 6:4 that says "There were giants in the Earth; and also after that . . ." indicates that maybe the "Sons of God" revisited the Earth after the flood and repeated their defiant acts on a smaller scale. Some Bible scholars believe that this is the origin of the race that produced Goliath and other "Giants".

In Deuteronomy 9:2, in the text of Moses' farewell to the Hebrew nation before they entered the Transjordon area, he said plainly that God's mission to them was to eliminate the Anakims race of giants that inhabited the land. It seems that God was determined to eliminate the offspring of the Sons of God from the Earth. The Anakims could only have been conceived after the flood by a second visit by the sons of God to mortal women.

Because of the contamination of the genes of the "Adamic" man, by the Sons of God, the whole "plan" was corrupted and had to be saved from destruction somehow. It was originally intended that Adam's race would mix with the lower primitive man on Earth to create a superior Homo sapiens. The visit of the "Sons of God" mixed the genes of Adams race with the superior

"Angels" that came down from God's domain. This union would have produced a race even superior to Adam. After this happened there was in Eden a menagerie of different kinds of man. There were the products of the Angels and Adams race, the products of the Angels and primitive man, primitive man himself, as well as Adams few remaining direct descendents. God knew that Eden and his "pure" race of Adam's descendants had been contaminated beyond recovery in all except Noah's family.

Consider the ramifications of a world populated by the descendants of this new race who were capable of overrunning and eliminating the weak existing population of the primitive man that lived outside Eden at that time. Ironically, according to science, it was Homo sapiens that suddenly appeared about 50,000 years ago as an advanced form of man and eventually overran and eliminated the Neanderthal man from the Earth around 26,000 BC.

God's "Plan" was not to eliminate this early form of man but to uplift him to new heights of civilization and morality in order to make him more acceptable for entrance into the "Kingdom of God", a term we will explore in a later chapter.

Noah was found "perfect" in his generation. The use of the word "perfect" was intended in a genetic sense, and did not refer to morality. His genetic line from Adam was without corruption from outside influence and was thus "perfect". That is why Noah was preserved through the great flood, so that God's "plan" for mankind could begin anew after the flood with Noah, who became in effect, the "new" Adam.

The only way to salvage the original plan was to destroy "man whom I have created from the face of the Earth". Notice that He does not say "All Man", but only the man "**that He created from the face of the Earth**", meaning, "that He had created in the garden". The first man was created by "letting the Earth bring forth", or through natural forces. The man, Adam, was created from the dust of the ground, or the "face of the Earth". God deliberately differentiated between the two forms of man in this statement.

Until I realized that there were indeed two forms of man on the Earth at that time, I thought that God was saying that He would destroy man and remove him from the Earth completely. This is another example of a simple phrase being misinterpreted quite innocently because we were missing some of the facts.

I would further suggest that whenever the Bible uses the phrase "*that He created*", it is referring only to the later creations, in the Garden, and does not include creations as a result of the first chapter of Genesis. That creation was of a different nature, different time, and was the result of God speaking things into being by saying, "Let the Earth bring forth . . .". Everything that resulted from that pronouncement was created as a result of the natural forces that God set up at the very beginning of the Universe. That is why the purpose of the Flood was to destroy all that He created at the second creation event in the Garden and not the first creation described in Genesis chapter one.

There is one other difference in the two creations that may be important. All things in the first creation were "spoken" into existence by God saying "LET . . .", and all things in the "Garden" creation were created "out of the ground" or from the "dust of the ground". God took elements that already existed, even genetic material from plants and animals, to use for the second creation.

In the first creation, when God created the Universe he created it from nothing. Even science admits now with what we are learning of Quantum mechanics, that it is possible to create matter from a total vacuum under the right conditions. It is not generally known that atomic particle creation from the nothingness of a vacuum is an everyday occurrence in the laboratories of particle physics. They say that the Universe happened because of a "quantum fluctuation" that "inflated" in the Big Bang. It is easy to label events and apply a "pseudo-explanation" of how it happened. The hard part is to answer the question of "why".

The second creation was different in that it didn't involve creating from nothing, but from taking existing elements and re-arranging their structure to make something new. That is another reason why the Bible speaks of "all that he created" as being a unique creation event separate from the first and more dramatic type of creation. The confusion for centuries is that we have tried to apply these words to everything from the beginning of time as one creation.

To further clarify this point, if I make a statement to someone that "the car that I bought was a lemon", I shouldn't have to explain that I'm talking about the LAST car that I bought. The listener should be intelligent enough to know that even though I have bought many cars through the years, I'm talking about the last car that I bought, not the first car I ever had. This is the same kind of argument I'm presenting here to explain what is meant when God says "all that I created". He means "the LAST time he created things on the Earth".

There is even reason to believe that after Adam and Eve left the garden, the Tree of Life may have been misused by the defiant "sons of God", because God also wanted to destroy all the animals created in the garden as well. He says in verse 12 "All flesh has corrupted His way on the Earth". If we interpret the phrase "*His way*" to mean "*His Plan for mankind*" then it suggests that what may have happened is that the Tree of Life had fallen into the wrong hands and life forms were generated that were not part of His plan in the beginning. These new, mutant life forms, as well as the offspring of the sons of God, were an abomination on the Earth and a corruption of God's plan. The result was the Flood.

Chapter Eleven

THE GREAT FLOOD

The situation in Eden had reached a climax with everything that God had created in the Garden having been changed by the defiant Sons of God, to mutant forms genetically, and even some new species being created that were not meant to be. When God looked over Eden and saw the corruption that had come from his Garden he must have been very upset. It is no surprise that he wanted to "destroy it all". Of all the men living in that region only Noah was still pure genetically and was a direct descendant from Adam. We can begin to see now the importance of preserving the genealogy of the direct line from Adam to certain individuals in the Bible. In fact the New Testament gives every individual in the line of Adam down to Jesus Christ. This level of detail is unusual and unexplained. Scholars have accepted that the Hebrew people felt it important to maintain an oral record of their lineage but no one has ever explained why.

This type of record-keeping is unique to these people and is not duplicated in any other race. The reason is that no other people had an original individual from which to trace their lineage and because of the mixing of the divine line of Adam with the primitive line of the outside world, the Hebrews understood the importance of being able to show that their lineage as a direct line from the first man, even though it was now mixed with the outside world genetically. This record shows that there was no corruption of genes by any of the "Sons of God that came down to Earth", in any of the descendants of Adam and the ancestry of Jesus.

This attention to detail is the reason why I believe that the book of Genesis pre-dates the records of the Sumerians and other ancient texts that scholars say are older than the Bible. The records were transmitted orally from one generation to another for over 2500 years until they had permanent written records given to them by Moses in the form of the first five books of the Old Testament.

God must have reasoned that if he destroyed everything in Eden he could start over with Noah and begin again with His original plan. He told Noah of the coming Flood and told him to prepare to save all the animals and plants he had created from the beginning of the Garden of Eden. These included only the strains of animals that had not been corrupted genetically by the Sons of God that came down. It also included the fruit trees and plants, and seeds of plants that he saw were "good to look at and to eat". He expected Noah to preserve his family and all these "creations" until after the destruction so that, in time, his descendants could fulfill the original plan, which was to take these "gifts" to primitive man and act as mentors in helping him to use them and become civilized.

In the book "Noah's Flood", by Ryan and Pittman, the actual event that caused the flood was said to be the rising of the Mediterranean until pressure caused a rift in the wall of the rim that grew larger and larger. The influx of water was said to be sudden and had the power of 200 Niagara Falls. Still, this would not explain how the water rose over the heights of the mountains surrounding this area. If this were the only cause of the flood, the water would only have risen to the level of the oceans beyond the rim of the Bosporus Strait.

There is one event that could have produced the cataclysmic flooding of the degree that Genesis describes, and still validate the evidence obtained by Ryan and Pitman.

My own theory of what happened is that a comet entered the atmosphere of the Earth, causing the rain to come down in quantities never before experienced by mankind. It hit in the ocean somewhere in the eastern Atlantic causing a giant wall of water that swept northward and eastward over Europe and the area of Eden, taking with it everything that was in its way. The force of the first shock wave caused the Bosporus Strait to breach and allowed the Mediterranean waters to pour into the Black Sea Basin, flooding and destroying all that lived within this 150,000 square mile area in a matter of hours. If the comet had hit the Mediterranean it would have destroyed all the colonies of primitive man living around it.

Further support is provided in the "Epic of Gilgamesh", a Sumerian tale of one of its kings, who on visiting the survivor of the great flood was told by him what happened just preceding the deluge.

> "Just as dawn began to glow there arose from the horizon a
> black cloud.
> Adad (lightning) rumbled inside of it,
> . . . setting the land ablaze with their flare.

> . . . the heavens, . . . turned to blackness all that had been
> light.
> The . . . land shattered like a . . . pot.
> All day long the South Wind blew . . . , blowing fast,
> submerging the mountain in water, overwhelming the people
> like an attack.
> No one could see his fellow, they could not recognize each other
> in the torrent."

This scenario describes perfectly what someone would see in this area if a comet had struck in the southern part of the Atlantic. The first sign would be a flash or glow on the horizon, followed by a rumbling of the earth. Then would follow a violent, hot wind created by the shock wave traveling through the atmosphere. The ground would be set ablaze for a short time while dust from the impact would blot out the sky and the sun. Finally the torrent of water from a mile high tsunami would come over the mountains and flood the basin.

We know that there was some flooding in the Fertile Crescent from a large deposit of clay discovered by George Smith, archeologist, in 1876 in the area between the Tigres and Euphrates, but little evidence of a major flood in other areas to the south. This indicates a wave of water that went in a northeastern direction from a point west and just south of Gibraltar. This would have lifted the ark of Noah up to the height that allowed it to be deposited on a mountaintop in the Ararat region. Ararat is about 100 miles east of the area described earlier as Eden. The Austrian Geologist and author, Alexander Tollman, who has written several articles of the possible effects of a comet impact on ancient civilizations, also holds to this theory concerning Noah's flood.

It is currently believed that remnants of Noah's ark still lie on the mountain named Ararat on the border between Turkey and the country of Armenia of the former Soviet Union. There are several popular books on the market outlining theories and expeditions to the modern day Mt. Ararat to see or try to recover artifacts from an object that was first seen during the First World War by Soviet pilots. This mountain is so high that it retains a snow cover and glacier the year around and is very difficult to scale, even when politics is favorable for an attempt.

The Bible describes the water as rising above the mountains and then receding. If this were a flood of worldwide proportions the rising of the oceans to that level would be permanent and the water would not recede because there would be no place to go. The Bible also says that the "windows of heaven were opened", and the "fountains of the deep broken up". This describes a comet impact like the one described above. In such a scenario the first event would be an enormous amount of rain as the comet entered the atmosphere over Europe and melted, accompanied by earthquakes and "fountains", or volcanoes, erupting and breaking up when the comet struck the ocean. Sumerian accounts of the flood suggest that a celestial object came to the Earth from the direction of the Pleiades, a constellation in the heavens, just before the flood. I believe that was the comet that caused the flood.

Of all the heavenly objects we know about, only comets are composed almost entirely of water in the form of ice. A comet of the size to affect the earth as I have described would be comparatively small, only 1-3 miles in diameter, about the size of a mountain. As the comet entered the atmosphere it would start to become hot and billions of tons of frozen water would instantly be vaporized and become part of the atmosphere. This increase in humidity would fall to Earth as a rain of proportions that had never been seen by man before or since. Easterly winds of Northern Europe would carry this humidity and rain over the continent and on into Siberia where it would come down as snow and ice.

It would take only minutes for the main body of the comet to impact the ocean and, perhaps within an hour, the wall of water about one mile high, from the main shock wave created by the impact would sweep over Europe going east as the greatest tsunami in history. As the Mediterranean would fill up from an initial increase in water it would then overflow the rim of the basin and break through the Bosporus Strait with great violence, just before the wall of water from the tidal wave would sweep over the mountains bringing instant destruction. This scenario would still be consistent with the archeological evidence for the flood as found by Ryan and Pitman. The basin would be flooded by water from the Mediterranean bursting through the Bosporus Strait, but just before a monster tidal wave swept away everything in its path. The tidal wave that went west toward America would have struck South America and also resulted in a catastrophic flood. There is recorded in Aztec records such an event, "when the world was flooded".

Noah's ark would probably have been built on a high level, probably in the highlands close to the original Garden of Eden, and would have been lifted up by the first water to enter the basin before the main wave hit. When the tidal wave came, the ark was probably pushed or carried along toward the East. Mt Ararat is directly east of the Black Sea and would have been the first high object in its path.

Robert Ballard, the head of the team that found the Titanic and other major deep water artifacts, is currently preparing to use the Deep Submergence Laboratory, to survey the bottom of the Black Sea in a series of dives. They have already documented the ancient coastline of

73

what was once a small freshwater lake before the flood, and found hints of human occupation along the shore. There are several renowned archaeologists in the group that will try to recover evidence of civilization in the area before the flood.

The exciting aspect of this project is the potential to recover items from the bottom that haven't aged in over 4000 years. The reason they haven't aged is due to the "anoxic" quality of the water below 650 feet. It doesn't contain oxygen and is the only such body of water in the world. Because there is no oxygen, things don't decay as they usually do in other bodies of water and in the atmosphere. The result is that artifacts that existed on the ancient, original coastline of the freshwater lake have been preserved in a condition that is very close to the way they were when they were covered by the flood.

If that is the truly the case, then the whole area of the basin has been preserved in a sort of "time capsule" that we may eventually be able to view for the first time since before Noah's lifetime.

According to Ballard, this project will occupy a great deal of his time for years to come. "I plan to be back in the Black Sea every summer," he says. "This is the beginning of the story, not the end."

After some time, the water left behind by the huge wave would run off into natural channels and back to the ocean. The Bible says that the waters eventually receded. This in itself indicates that the cause of the flood was a wave of water and not a permanent rise in the amount of water. Its effects must have reached well into northern Asia because there have been mammoths and other animals discovered recently, frozen in ice in a standing position, with fresh grass in their stomachs. This suggests that they were frozen in their tracks. The cold of northern Russia would have almost frozen the water instantly. The part of the comet that broke up in the atmosphere would have come down in that area as a tremendous snow storm instead of rain, creating an instant glacier trapping the animals almost before they knew what was happening.

It could be said that the flood was worldwide in that every part of the world would have felt its impact in some form. The tidal wave would have swept around the globe, though not as powerfully as it did in Western Europe and the area around Eden. The impact and earthquakes would have triggered volcanic activity in every unstable area.

The aftermath of the flood would have been total destruction in the area of Eden and for several hundred miles beyond. The event as viewed by primitive man everywhere except in the direct path of the shockwave, would be felt as an earthquake followed by the swift rising of the waters locally, and in the ocean for a short time, then everything returning to normal.

Where the basin of Eden and a fresh water lake once existed there was now a vast salty sea filled with dead freshwater life that could not survive in the salt water that came in from the Mediterranean. To this day there is no life in the Black Sea below 250 feet below the surface due to the toxicity of dead animal and plant life that still remains below that level. Of all that existed in Eden before the flood, only Noah and his ark remained.

Chapter Twelve

A New Beginning

After the Flood, Noah and his family were visited by God and they entered into a Covenant that said never again would He destroy man using a flood. The rainbow was to be a reminder that man was now under the care and protection of God and his forces. The plan was back on track. Because of the tremendous amount of water left on earth by the comet, the climate of the earth was changed worldwide. Locally around the present Black Sea area the climate changed from a dry, arid climate to a more humid state that enjoyed plentiful rainfall, whereas before there was none. Because of the change in climate, rainbows were now possible in this area for the first time since before the ice age.

I'm sure that Noah was told what to do with the seeds, the plants, the animals, and other "gifts" that God had prepared for the "other', "primitive" man to have. His mission was now to "Be fruitful and multiply, and replenish the Earth", Genesis 9:1. This was an order to replace the population existing outside the flooded area, with the new line of Noah that was "pure".

It would take several generations before the numbers of Noah's descendants would be great enough to accomplish God's mission. It would have taken years of care and replanting for enough seeds to be produced for Noah's descendents to accomplish the task that God had assigned to them. These would be the fruits of Eden that would be shared with the rest of the world.

Genesis 9:21 says "And Noah began to be an husbandman, and he planted a vineyard." This is the first record of grapes being grown anywhere. Even scholars today who have studied the beginnings of certain plants agree that the grape was first found in the area around Mount Ararat in Georgia, and spread from there to other areas of the world.

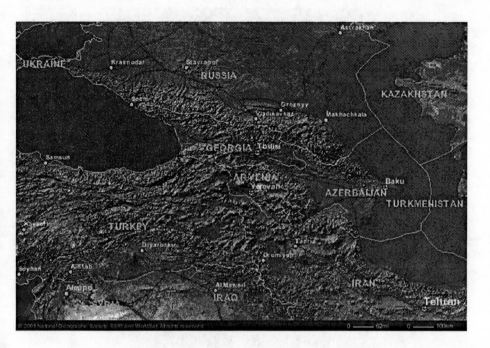

The Area of Ararat and Georgia

We know that the Sumerians were visited by Noah's descendants while Noah was still alive because a Sumerian story of it's fifth King, Gilgamesh, indicates that he was a great-great grandson of the one who came through the great flood, whether that be Noah or one of his sons. Noah lived for three hundred and fifty years after the flood. His son Shem lived 600 years in all and lived well into the life span of Abraham.

It appears from the Bible that after several generations, most of Noah's descendants came to settle in one area called Shinar and there began a city that was composed almost entirely of their family or offspring

There must have been a small settlement of primitive man there at the time, who saw the visitors as powerful Gods who were knowledgeable about all things. A tale from the *"Legends of the Bible"* and a passage in Genesis 10:9 tells us that Nimrod was the first King or leader to exercise great power and influence in the area. He was the first King of Shumer, or Sumer as we have come to know it. It was at his direction that the tower of Babel was begun.

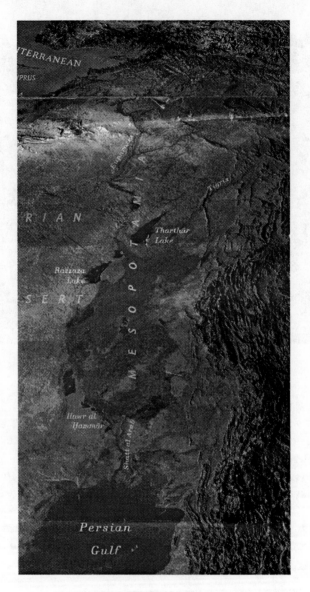

The Plains of Shinar

Tradition has it that he possessed a garment that was worn by Adam that protected him from harm of any kind. It was supposedly handed down through Noah and his descendants to him. It is told that he was an ungodly man who was corrupted with the power that the garment gave him. The Bible describes him as the first man to be known as "Mighty".

There is no record of any other city-state or country of power anywhere in the world at this time. Mankind consisted of many disjointed bands of hunter-gatherers or primitive farmers, and no colony was yet large enough to achieve the status of what we would call an organized power. The city of Shumer was the first brick and mortar city and military power on the face of the Earth. Nimrod's reign was the first example of an advanced civilization ever recorded.

We don't know how long the city of Shumer existed before they decided to build a tower but the Bible states that they began immediately to build from brick and mortar. As soon as the tower of Babel was begun God said that it must be stopped.

It is very important to stop here and try to determine why God took the action he did and caused them to be dispersed. The Bible says that he "confounded their language" and caused them to be dispersed.

They had said, "Let us make for us a name". It was clearly their purpose to unite and form a nation under the "name", just as our countrymen broke away from Britain 200 years ago and said, "Let us form a nation under the name of The United States". A name for a nation indicates a unity of purpose and helps to draw the people together.

We must realize that the inhabitants of Shumer, or Sumer were all direct descendants of Noah and Adam. God was concerned that they would be so powerful and advanced that they would eventually threaten the existence of the "other" man who was not so capable. It's no wonder that God said, "Now nothing will be restrained from them which they have imagined to do."

How capable were they? They were all descendants of Noah who was a direct descendant of Adam. They had extremely long life spans, were highly intelligent, possessing skills in agriculture, metalworking, building materials, and other skills that the inferior Homo sapiens man did not have, and probably, that we still do not yet have, even today.

It was never God's intention from the beginning of the Garden to allow the descendants of Adam to unite and form a super race or nation of their own. Collectively, they had the intellect and superior knowledge to create a civilization that could well have exceeded our own present day technology within a short time if they were allowed to continue. God's intended purpose for them was to carry the seeds of the new form of wheat and other crops, knowledge of agriculture, the fruit trees, and animals that were created in the garden, and themselves to the areas of the world where mortal man lived and help him to advance. That was why God had to scatter them in all directions.

The way he accomplished this was brilliant. It is likely that they were already assigned to an area, and had orders to travel to that land and mix in with the population already in that area. I believe that He made each of them begin to talk in the language of the primitive colonies of people they were supposed to visit and help. They could not understand each other and could only communicate if they continued to journey until they found the people they were supposed to give the "gifts" of Eden to. It's even possible that representatives of God told they how to find the people that spoke their new language. Thus they were forced to continue the "plan".

Another of the earliest cities of the plain to rise, besides Sumer and Babylon, was the city of Ur of the Chaldees, a very early civilization. This was perhaps 300-400 years after the flood. If that seems like a short time for all these civilizations to spring up, consider that our own country is only a little over 200 years old and that our own civilization was still very primitive just 100 short years ago compared to the present.

Ur was the home of one of the lines of Shem, Noah's oldest son. The genealogy went as follows: Shem, Ar-phax'ad, Sa'lah, Eber (from who the Hebrew got their name), Pe'leg, Re'u, Se'rug, Nahor, Te'rah, and Abram (Abraham). Abraham was only 15 generations removed from Adam the first Man. All of the life spans from Adam to Noah were constant with an average lifespan of about 900 to 950 years.

When God told Adam that the day he ate of the fruit of the tree of knowledge of good and evil he would die, he was true to his word. If a day to God is as a thousand years to us, according to 2 Peter 3:8 in the New Testament, then Adam and his descendants actually lived less than one day by God's reasoning.

From Noah on, the life spans begin to decrease in step-like fashion. It is interesting to look at the life spans of these individuals as the generations became more distant from their ancestor, Noah.

Shem lived 600 years
Ar-phax'ad lived 438 years
Sa'lah lived 433 years
Eber lived 464 years
Pe'leg lived 239 years
Re'u lived 239 years
Se'rug lived 230 years
Na'hor lived 149 years
Te'rah lived 205 years
Abram lived 175 years

LIFESPANS: NOAH TO JACOB

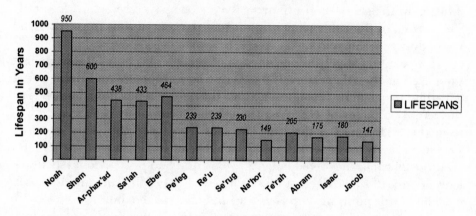

The decreases in lifespan are almost in a geometric progression. Every fourth generation saw a significant drop to a lower plateau until with Jacob and the following generations, the life span begins to be closer to the 120 years predicted by God before the flood. By 4 generations after Abraham the life spans were in the 100-120 year range.

This unusual phenomenon can be explained by the descendants of Noah taking wives of primitive man whose life span was a mere 35-40 years at that time. By mixing their genes with the inferior man, the offspring would have a lifespan somewhat more than the mother's and less than the father's. It is clear that within 10 generations of Noah, man's lifespan had dropped from around 900 years to the neighborhood of 140 years.

It was very important to the Hebrew people that they keep a record of every individual's line of descent from Adam. Every family kept meticulous records of their genealogy and were religious in making sure that every offspring knew it by heart. I believe they did this because it was important to them early in their history to show that they were descendants of Adam and Noah, and had their genes in their blood. At the time when much of the world still had remnants of the primitive man still living, to do so meant to be of royal blood.

Scientists may argue that the genes of one man, Adam or Noah would be so diluted in the infusion into the bloodline of millions of Homo sapiens that it would have no effect on the life spans of their descendants.

I would use the argument that they have used for so long against people of faith to explain away man's creation by God. Evolution would make it so.

The argument would go this way: Noah lived 950 years and had 3 sons who each lived several hundreds of years. Each of those sons lived long enough to have possibly a hundred or more children. Because of dilution of the genes their offspring lived successively shorter life spans. The record in the Bible shows that it took 10 generations to go from 950 years down to 150 years.

If we conservatively allow for each of Noah's sons only 50 sons during their lifetime then there were 150 sons by Shem, Japheth, and Ham. To get a method to calculate from, lets assume that every generation decreases in lifespan by a factor of 1/2, even though the records say it decreased less than that. That means that the 150 sons lived only 450 years and had proportionately fewer sons, only 25 each, because of less time to procreate. Of those 25 each, they lived only 225 years and had proportionately fewer sons of only 12 each. Each of those sons lived only 150 years and had only 6 each. At this point we stop counting and analyze the data.

Given that we have been overly conservative in the number of children possible by each generation, (I had a great grandfather who had 23 children), and we used life spans that were much shorter than those given in the Bible, and that the sons had daughters also, let us calculate the results for the 5 generations to see how many offspring there would be. The mathematics is as follows: $50 \times 25 \times 12 \times 6 = 270,000$ sons in the fifth generation alone, not counting daughters of equal numbers, and not counting over 55,000 still living from previous generations.

The total population of the inferior Homo sapiens was probably 10-20 million at that time and it seems that perhaps numbers alone would overwhelm the 270,000, but remember that evolution says that the fittest survive. When you consider that Adam and Noah had to be immune to diseases to live as long as they did, and their descendants had to have some of that immunity also, it is reasonable to say that Noah's descendants did not die in infancy as often as the inferior Homo sapiens man did. With 270,000 offspring who are genetically protected from most diseases that take infants from the inferior Homo sapiens members, and by taking wives of that species, they would produce in the next generation over a million offspring that would still live three times longer than the existing primitive man due to physical and genetic makeup.

Also the inferior man, by only living a third of the lifespan of the descendants of Noah, would have fewer children and would lose many of those to disease. The next generation would see the proportion of people who could call themselves descendants of Noah in the total population of man, approach 50 percent. This is after only 6 generations. Remember that our own country has had less than 10 generations born to it since it was founded.

In time the weaker man would become proportionately less and less of the total population just by evolutionary forces acting on a weaker sector of the species. Assuming that each succeeding generation has only 5 sons, a reasonable number given the propensity for large families at that time for farming purposes, after 9 generations the strain of primitive man that existed before the flood would cease to exist for all practical purposes. However, as the Noah's line becomes more removed from their patriarch, they become more susceptible to disease and infant death, though never to the extent that primitive man once was.

The following chart is based on a conservative estimate of the impact of Noah's line on the existing population of man.

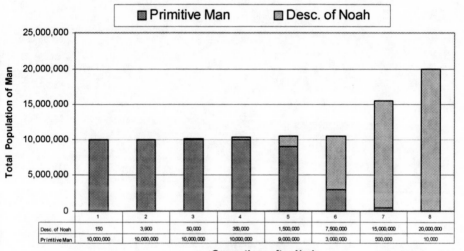

NOAH'S DESCENDANTS AS A PROPORTION OF THE TOTAL POPULATION OF MAN

	1	2	3	4	5	6	7	8
Desc. of Noah	150	3,900	50,000	350,000	1,500,000	7,500,000	15,000,000	20,000,000
Primitive Man	10,000,000	10,000,000	10,000,000	10,000,000	9,000,000	3,000,000	500,000	10,000

Generations after Noah

As the pure primitive, weaker strain of man died out, the lifespan of the remaining sector would approach 120 years maximum, not allowing for disease and accidents. As the proportion of the population that is of the line of Noah increases, the total population will grow due to the increased longevity and a strengthened resistance to disease and death. We have people who have lived that long today, but the 120 years predicted by God in Genesis 6:3 still seems to be the maximum for anyone.

Because of their long life span, the earlier generations probably actually outlived many wives and had hundreds of children. These would work their way into the gene pools of the civilizations they visited and slowly the lifespan of a large portion of the primitive man's total population was increased. From this point on, the word "Man" could apply to anyone on the Earth. There would be no one left who could say that he didn't have some of Adam's blood in him.

In this way the genes of the first "Man" of the Garden of Eden, Adam, were finally absorbed into the population of the primitive Homo sapiens man of the rest of the world.

I think it is appropriate to say at this point that everyone living today has some of the genes of Adam after 5000 years of intermixing within the species. We are all descendants of Adam, the first "man", except for a few individuals that I know personally, that I am sure are the last remnants of the Neanderthal line.

Chapter Thirteen

THE SEVEN SAGES

The kingdom of Sumer is accepted by all historians as the oldest civilization on Earth for which there are any records. No one knows where the Sumerians came from according to the archeological records. The Bible in Genesis 11:2 says "And it came to pass, as men journeyed from the east, they found a plain in the land of Shinar; and they settled there." The word "Shinar" is an ancient name for Shumer or Sumer. The misspelling came about when Dr. George Smith accidentally copied "Sumer" instead of Shumer in the reporting of his findings while digging there in the last century. Where archeology fails to find evidence of previous habitation the Bible provides an explanation of where they came from.

Tradition has it that after the flood Noah and his family came to settle around the mountain known today as Ararat on the border between Turkey and the former Soviet Union. This mountain is about 100 miles east of the area I have proposed as the Eden in the Bible. When Noah's sons settled and had families of their own, the descendants of Noah began to multiply until their numbers were such as to begin to migrate to the west in search of more and better land to settle. The plain of the Mesopotamia, between the Tigris and the Euphrates rivers was an oasis surrounded by desert and mountains.

Consider the reaction of a primitive tribe who probably was already living in this area of "Shinar," to suddenly being visited by beings who spoke their language, who were probably very much older than themselves, and had knowledge of things they considered "magical".

When the descendants of Noah first encountered the inhabitants of the plain of Shinar they must have appeared as God-like beings to these primitives. According to ancient Sumerian clay texts the first inhabitants of Sumer were visited by 7 "sages" who taught them how to grow crops, make and fire bricks for construction, establish government, and other skills necessary for an advanced civilization. Does the fact that Noah's sons and grandchildren lived to be hundreds of years old have anything to do with the word "Sage" here? Consider the importance of this encounter.

This was the beginning of agriculture, the skill that all historians consider was the most necessary development for civilization to become a reality. My suggestion, and belief, is that these "sages" were 7 descendants of Noah who were among the first to migrate from the Ararat landing of the Ark of Noah to the western areas where civilizations sprang up.

There is much evidence that agriculture did spread also over Europe and outward from the Black Sea area in the centuries after the flood, according to research documented in *Noah's Flood*. However, Ryan and Pitman attribute this to skills spread by human survivors of the flood who migrated outward when their homeland was flooded. They offer no explanation for how these survivors acquired this knowledge of agriculture or the crops that suddenly appeared.

My hypothesis is that the spread of agriculture was due to one family, Noah's descendants, who preserved the knowledge of agriculture and fruits of the Garden specifically for this dispersion.

Other areas where advanced civilizations appeared were Egypt, Assyria, Babylon, Greece, Eurich and other city-states that suddenly and almost overnight, simultaneously, developed languages, forms of writing, and other evidence of advanced lifestyles.

When the Egyptian Hieroglyphics were first discovered it was thought that they were an original written language form. It has since been discovered that it is really a form of the written language that began in Sumer. Recent discoveries and scientific thought has brought many historians to the conclusion that in almost every case, the written languages of the earliest civilizations can be traced or seen to contain some elements of the Sumerian written language. No evidence exists anywhere of a civilization, a language, or a written record that existed before the Sumerians.

It seems natural to assume that everywhere one or several of the descendants of Noah appeared the inhabitants adopted them as Gods and accepted them as the leader of their people. The Bible says that Ham's descendants went to Egypt, Ethiopia, and Northern African nations, the second area where great civilizations suddenly made the leap to civilization. It was from the city of Ur that the descendants of Shem and Eber, Abraham and the Hebrew people came. According to all archeological and historical data, except in the Bible, the origin of the Semitic people is a mystery.

The Sumerians kept a record of their leaders called the "Kings List", in which they recorded their names and lengths of rein. They all apparently had long life spans of hundreds of years. Gilgamesh was the fifth king in the list, and in his "epic" that we referred to earlier, he admits to being a descendant of the survivor of the "great flood". I believe that all the first "kings" of Sumer were directly descended from Noah and that is how they came to have the attribute of long lives. A curious thing about the "Kings List" is that each succeeding king had a shorter rein than the proceeding one. This could be explained by intermarrying with the inhabitants of the plain, with each generation becoming further removed from Noah's pure line, diluting the longevity genes of their ancestor Noah.

In the "Epic of Gilgamesh" the main character, on learning of his ancestry, which included the "Gods" who came through the great flood, decides to find out if he will live a normal lifespan or the lifespan of his ancestors. To find out, he has to find someone who knows where to find the "Gods", to ask them. He finally is told that the answer lies at the "Gateway to Life" which contains the "Tree of Life". He travels a long journey that included following the Euphrates River back into the mountains and finally comes upon "an enclosure of the Gods" wherein there "grew" a garden made up entirely of precious stones. He describes beautiful trees of every kind of fruit and beauty. He mentions the "Tree of Life", but the clay tablets are damaged at this point and we do not know what happened next.

The story continues at a later point with Gilgamesh finally finding his ancestor who came through the flood. This was either Noah or one of his sons. He asks how to get eternal life and is told that because he is of mortal blood he cannot obtain that, but he can postpone death by obtaining a certain plant, which the Gods themselves eat to remain young.

During Gilgamesh's journey he had to cross a large body of water called the "Sea of Death". I believe that this is the Black Sea just after the flood. When the salty Mediterranean poured into the basin of the fresh water lake it would have killed all life contained in the lake and surrounding it. Considering that God used the flood to destroy all the descendants of the "Sons of God and daughters of men" affair, it would have become a "Sea of Death" for all within the walls of the basin. We today call that area the Black Sea. As previously mentioned, even today no life can exist below 250 feet below the water's surface.

The "Gods", who Gilgamesh sought to learn of the secret of life, were probably either the sons of Noah or the first generation descendants of them, who were still alive at that time. They were revered because of their long life spans. As each generation of sons after Noah would marry mortal wives they would lose some of the qualities of their parents and the God-like properties would die out after a great number of generations.

A side note to this is that some of the sons of Noah and their sons probably outlived many of the later generations whose life spans fell drastically to the levels of mortal man. One case was Shem, Noah's oldest son who lived 600 years and was alive during the lifetime of Abraham, 6 generations later, who lived 175 years. It is believed that he was also the priest called Melchizedech, who was revered by Abraham so much that he paid tithes to him.

The Greeks were another civilization that was highly advanced in their philosophy and social skills. They also went to great lengths to reward and recognize athletic skills as well. The first Olympics were begun to celebrate physical and athletic prowess. History and writings tell of Greek Gods who preceded the civilization of Greece, Gods, some of whom were offspring of other Gods and mortal men. One of these, Hercules, was supposed to be the strongest man on Earth. How hard is it to draw the conclusion that this tale began from one or more of Noah's descendants who visited the land long before, exhibited superior mental and physical skills that they had never seen before, and told stories of a time when "Gods came down to Earth and had children by mortals". I believe that many of the myths of ancient Greece had their origin in the period when the descendants of Noah were active in the post diluvium world after the flood.

If God's plan was to help Homo sapiens make the leap from the Stone Age into civilization by providing superior leaders and technology at a critical time in his development, it was succeeding through the descendants of Noah.

Chapter Fourteen

OTHER NATIONS, OTHER GODS

Throughout this book the central theme has been that all that we have today is the result of a movement that can be traced back to a very short time in history when man experienced a technological explosion, and it began with one tiny city-state with a very few inhabitants. This could only have happened with very special people who had extraordinary abilities, and a mission to use those abilities to affect history.

It is likely that every nation and people on the Earth today owes those individuals a debt of gratitude for what we have achieved. You might ask how so few could affect so many in such a profound way as to influence their art, culture, language, and yes, even their religion. The following description is pure speculation as to what happened, based on some supporting scientific data and the account as given in chapter 10 of the book of Genesis. It seems to be the only one around and until someone gives me a better explanation I will cling to it.

After the disaster at the Tower of Babel the inhabitants had no choice but to scatter to find people who they could communicate with. There must have been a circle of individuals who knew of God's ultimate plan and were loyal and determined to see that it succeeded. They provided the organization, the design, and the assignments to other, equally capable descendants of Noah, who were willing to carry the gifts and the message of God to all parts of the Earth. We have to remember that only two generations after Noah, his descendants would have numbered in the hundreds.

They fully realized that their mission was to go, probably alone, to the far corners of the Earth, wherever primitive Homo sapiens had settled, and infiltrate their culture, and use the products of the Garden of Eden, and their own genetic constitution, to create a new species of man. This new man would be gifted with enhanced abilities in symbolic reasoning, artistic endeavors, agriculture, and a higher form of civilization. They knew all too well that they would be seen as Gods and that for the plan to succeed, they must intermix with the population in such a way that they would have many offspring from which a new gene pool would be created. This is why many of the earlier kings of Egypt, Greece, Babylon, Sumer, and all the ancient classical cultures of the third millennium B.C. have records of rulers who were either divine, or interestingly, part-God.

If a person's father was considered a God, what reason would they have then to claim to be "part God"? The answer is that they knew that their father had a wife who was not of the same Godly lineage that their father was, and this could only happen if the fathers were in fact beings who were very different and superior in abilities to the normal inhabitants.

All through the records of ancient civilizations we find references to rulers who were ½ God or 1/4 God, who were clinging to some claim to divine ancestry. Why would a person ruling a powerful nation claim to be only ½ God unless there was some basis that was known by the general population? The basis was that they had all seen the "visitors" from the Mesopotamia area who were revered for their abilities and were considered Gods, who had been the fathers of many children who had a mortal mother.

On reading the Book of the Mormons for the first time, I was struck by the statement in the beginning that the ancestors of the Native Americans were a group of people called the Lamanites who were among the multitudes scattered at the Tower of Babel. The story goes that the Lamanites came to what is now America and brought civilization and knowledge to the local, primitive inhabitants, just as in the other accounts. This fits in well with my contention that the event at the Tower of Babel resulted in the dispersing of the fruits of the Garden of Eden to all corners of the Earth.

There are even later accounts of other encounters of the American Indians with "visitors" from across the seas. The Incas of Central and South American were conquered by Cortez and the Spanish only because they thought he was the return of the strange "white man" Quetzacoatl who had visited them centuries earlier and brought to them knowledge and civilization. The Aztecs of Mexico even had a legend of a great flood in which the only survivor was a man named Noe, a name very similar to the biblical Noah.

How did they journey so far with so little technology 4,500 years ago? You have to understand that they had abilities and knowledge that were above what the science books of today claim man had at that time. These were the descendants of a superior race of man that was created from the dust by God in the Garden of Eden. They did not have the genes of the "Homo sapiens" man of our science books. They did not get their intelligence from evolutionary forces in excruciatingly small steps as Homo Erectus, Neanderthal, and even the Homo sapiens man did, over the past 2 million years. Their ancestry could be traced in Genesis directly back to God himself.

Following this logic, it can be assumed that they were far superior to even present day man in intelligence. We are today a very diluted version of that race of man because we are the offspring of the union between their kind and the very much inferior Homo sapiens of our science books.

There is a curious tale about Sarah, the wife of Abraham, in *"Legends of the* Bible" by Louis Ginzberg that Sarah was so beautiful compared to the Egyptian women when Abraham went down to Egypt, that Egyptian women looked like apes beside her. Perhaps the originators of this story were closer to the truth than they realized.

There are other stories and traditions handed down by the Hebrews that when Adam died his body did not decay. These stories also hold for the direct descendants of Adam all the way down to 2 or 3 generations after Noah. It is said that even Abraham didn't look old until just before his death. After that began the trait that the Hebrew book *"Legends of the Bible"* call the "lingering death" in which men started looking old long before their time to die of old age, as we do today. Only at that time did their bodies start showing the traits of normal humans by decaying at their death.

Menes, who, legends have it, traveled to Egypt from the Mesopotamia region, and demonstrated superior skills organizing and running the royal granaries, began the first dynasty of Egypt. As a result of his prowess in management, he rose to become the ruler of Egypt. He lived longer than any previous monarch and claimed to be descended from the Gods themselves. His children retained their father's powers of strength and longevity because they too exhibited these unique abilities. This began the practice of revering the ruler of Egypt as divine, and his succeeding family members began the great dynasties of Egypt. The first generations after Menes took pride in their claim to be ½ God or ¼ God, because as their fathers took wives of the inhabitants, they could no longer claim pure divinity.

The Pyramids were probably an attempt to preserve the bodies of later rulers in the same way that the earlier rulers were preserved naturally. Because the bodies of Noah and his descendants did not decay the way inferior humans did, the inhabitants of Egypt took this as a sign of divinity. His direct descendants would surely have the same characteristic to some degree.

This became the mark of someone truly divine to the ancient Egyptians, and all succeeding generations wanted to prove that they too were divine by having bodies that did not decay. To not be divine became an embarrassment to later rulers, so much so, that they went to extremes to prevent the populace from finding out.

After many generations in which rulers became less like Adam and more like mortal man, maintaining this illusion proved difficult. As a result, the rulers began long before their death to prepare a special place where none of the elements of the earth that caused decay, could penetrate. The first pyramids were small, stepped structures that were eventually broken into by thieves. The people could see that the ruler did indeed decay and efforts were made to take more drastic steps to preserve the body and keep anyone from seeing the body. To further guarantee that the body would be preserved, they learned that certain herbs and medicines would help to keep the body from decaying. This began the practice of mummifying the body. The rulers believed that divine bodies that did not decay would eventually go on to Heaven and continue life there. If they decayed, they believed that they would not be able to continue life.

The historians of today claim that mummifying the body and building Pyramids were simply religious practices and part of a ritual to help the ruler make the transition to heaven. They are missing the point, that the people had actually witnessed earlier, actual evidence that "true" Gods did not decay at death, and were probably told by them that there was a place where they would go to after death. They simply wanted to emulate what they had seen earlier with their own eyes.

The great pyramid of Giza is nothing more than the latest, greatest attempt to surround the body of the Pharaoh with so much material, at a position so high above the ground, which was considered the source of decay, that he would be preserved forever. It also served a second equally important purpose in sealing the body from prying eyes. They reasoned that by surrounding the body by massive amounts of stone the elements could not penetrate and cause decay. If, however, this did not work, at least the inhabitants could not get in to see that they were very human and were not, in fact, divine after all.

One interesting character in Egyptian history is the man named Imhotep. He is given credit as the architect of the first pyramid, the author of literary and medical texts, the chief advisor to King Djoser, and was revered by Egyptians as a "God of wisdom". His abilities and talents seem strikingly similar to those of the "God-like visitors" that I discussed earlier. He has been dated to have lived in the middle of the Third Millennium BC.

The March, 2001 issue of Astronomy Magazine included a short article that the Egyptians had used two heavenly objects in alignment with the North Star, Polaris to construct the pyramid in a way that aligned the great pyramid of Kufu at Giza to true north. Because of a slight error in their calculations it is now possible to determine the exact date construction began. That date is now suggested to be 2478 BC.

With a population of probably a million inhabitants in the area that later became Egypt, what kind of attributes would a man need to be called a God? Historians would have us believe that everyone who was above average in some field was considered a "God" by the ancient peoples, but I don't think that this honor was given so casually. For an entire nation to think of any man as a God, he would have to be so far above anyone else that there would be no comparison. I believe that they had good reasons to consider these individuals as a form of "God".

The construction of the other Pyramids was the work of later geniuses. Great engineering and knowledge of construction methods went into their construction. Where did that knowledge come from in such a short time? It is a pity that so much fruitless effort was made just to try to emulate something that they had observed earlier, the ability of a person's body to die and not decay.

The Greek civilization has long been recognized as one of the most advanced, most civilized, and learned, of the entire ancient world. It reached its zenith around 323 B.C. under Alexander the Great.

They had legends and myths that are still being played out today on stage and movie screen. The legends of their superheroes, such as Atlas, Hercules, and Prometheus are seen daily on television and movie re-runs. These tales have survived for over 3000 years and continue to raise questions as to their origin.

It is the belief of this author that the heroes of ancient Greece were the descendants of Noah, 2 or 3 generations removed. The Greeks consider the founder of their people to be a man named Deucalion, who created numerous towns and temples.

According to *World Mythology* written by Roy Willis, the Greeks had a tale or belief that in man's history he had progressed through 5 different races. The best-known version of this tale was told by Hesiod in *Works and Days*.

This tale records that the first race of man was called the Golden Race, whose members did not suffer from old age, sickness or toil. This sounds like Adam and his direct descendants down to Noah. Adam was born into a garden paradise that should provided him with everything he needed, had he not been cast out.

The second race was the Silver Race, who took a century to mature and was arrogant and violent, and did not worship God. This sounds like the race of man that was created when the Sons of God took wives of the daughters of men, as told in the Bible. Genesis 6:11 says, "The Earth also was corrupt before God, and the Earth was filled with violence." Their fate according to the tale was to continue to inhabit the underworld as spirits

The third race was the Bronze Race. They were responsible for learning metalworking and building civilization. This would correspond to the first descendants of the sons of Noah who, according to Genesis 10, introduced brick making and built the first city on the plains of Shinar (Sumer), before the Tower of Babel incident scattered them.

The fourth race was the Race of Heroes, who were born of divine fathers and human mothers. This is exactly the scenario that I described earlier that took place immediately after the Tower of Babel, when his descendants were scattered to the winds. Wherever they settled, they were revered as Gods and took wives of the primitive mortal women in that area. Their sons would have had some of the abilities of their "divine" fathers but were also mortal. To the backward people who lived in the area they were "Heroes" or supermen who had strength and abilities beyond anything they had ever seen before. These became the Heroes of Greece that we read about in Homer's stories and college textbooks on Greek Mythology.

The fifth race was the Race of Iron, which included the modern line of the human race. After the genes and abilities of the "Heroes" mixed with the ordinary line of humans, it took several generations for the mixture to stabilize on a new race of man that was created below the "Gods and Heroes" of Greek legends but had abilities above the previous race of humans that inhabited the land before the "Gods" came. That race of humans is representative of the line we are all a part of today.

Given the previous narrative and my explanation of the origin of modern man, it would be accurate to say that the race of man that exists today did not exist before 2500 B.C., and actually did begin in the Garden of Eden with Adam and Eve.

I could not have described the development of the human race better than the Greeks did in their "Five Races" tale. It includes every different being that existed from Adam down to modern man. Even though it comes from Greek mythology it corresponds very closely with the biblical account of man, and my hypothesis that the "Biblical" man mixed with the primitive Homo sapiens to create a new race of man that we now call "modern man". The Greeks were revered by all civilizations at their highest as being the wisest of cultures and spawning the greatest thinkers. I don't think even our opinions today do justice to the knowledge and wisdom that they actually did have.

There was a library in Alexandria, Egypt that lasted approximately 800 years. It was composed of 400,000 scrolls and documents that were supposed to include all the known history and knowledge of the world at that time. The city of Alexandria was founded in honor of Alexander the Great, in Egypt, and was considered to be the center of the known world. It was placed there because of the apparent stability and safety of that region of the world at that time. All important texts were taken there and stored for safe-keeping. It was known as the greatest storehouse of human knowledge in the world. The curators of the library went to great lengths to be sure that either the original or a copy of every written document in the world was stored in it in some form. Even the shipping lists of trading ships were saved as soon as a ship docked. They mistakenly thought that the safest place for that knowledge was in one archive under the protection of the most civilized nation on Earth at that time.

One of the greatest tragedies in the history of man was the destruction of that library in 415 A.D. by Cyril, Theophilus' nephew, who succeeded him as Patriarch of Christianity for the Roman Empire. Many of the most ancient documents concerning the early rise of civilization were lost forever because they were considered heretical. Today, several diggings where the library stood have revealed scientific and historical documents, which show that had the library survived, the industrial revolution would have occurred 1500 years earlier, according to Ellen Brundige in *The Decline of the Library and Museum of Alexandria*, December 10, 1991.

Among the lost documents included were descriptions of the methods used to build the pyramids. The papyrus scrolls, all 400,000, were used as fuel to heat the baths of the conquering Roman bands. What could we have known today about that period for which there is so little information, if only those documents had survived? It was as if all history of man was destroyed at that point and had to start anew.

This event was one of the significant events triggering what we now call the "Dark Ages". One of the main differences between man and beast is his ability to store knowledge for later generations to benefit from. Take away that tool and every generation would begin again from the ground floor of civilization as barbarians. It is truly an accurate description for that time because we forgot, perhaps forever to some extent, who we are and where we came from, with the loss of those records. We have recovered some of that history, but we are still in the "dark" about many aspects of it. There is a 2000-year "gap" of information about our history that we can only speculate about.

How much would a future world know about our civilization today if all historical records were destroyed due to an atomic war, and civilization fell back to the level of the Stone Age? Suppose that at some future time man found his way back to civilization and a technological culture, and tried to piece together the history of his species. Suppose that with no records or documents he had to rely only on artifacts that had survived the war. How much could he know about our civilization, our culture, and our history, from looking at only inscriptions on granite or marble monuments, statues, and parts of buildings that had survived?

That is what we are trying to do today, and artifacts, monuments, and a scant few documents are all that we have to work with. Had the records that were in the Library of Alexandria survived we could have seen what was probably common knowledge for the citizens of that age, that our rise to civilization was not a haphazard, random event as portrayed by our history and science books. The Jewish historian Josephus, who wrote *The Antiquities of the Jews* after their fall to the Roman Empire, in 70 A.D., wrote of the Ark of Noah and the flood as if it were common knowledge to all citizens, including the Romans.

The loss of this library is one of the reasons for the huge gap in our information chain of man for the period just after the Flood of Noah. The only detailed records surviving are the tablets found in the ancient Sumerian library and the Bible, and many historians discount or ignore those accounts altogether, because they describe events that couldn't possibly be true because they go against "common sense". They are simply "religious artifacts"

Chapter Fifteen

THE ORIGIN OF RELIGIONS

Probably the most important time in human history was the short 300 year period of 2500-2200 B.C. discussed earlier, a time during which the inhabitants of Mesopotamia area defined our present world, our values, introduced agriculture, metal working, government, the building of cities, and set the course of civilization for the next 6000 years. Quite an accomplishment for a small number of people in an area less than 500 miles wide!

I believe that this is also the period of time during which most of the world's religions were founded. To some who have read this far, this book may seem an attempt to disregard other religions and beliefs but that is not the purpose here. I hope to suggest and to show that religion is not an inherent characteristic of man, as some historians and anthropologists imply, and that most beliefs in a hereafter and a supreme intelligence can actually be traced back to a common origin.

It is easy, by listening to news commentators, to get the idea that all religions around the world are evenly distributed and are equally valid, according to the numbers of followers, when in truth over half the world's population worships one unique God. Regardless of what they call Him, the Muslims, Jews, and Christians all serve the same God, the God of a man named Abraham. These three faiths comprise over 3.7 billion people on Earth. There are 2.5 billion Christians, 1.2 billion Muslims, and 16 million Jews. With over half the world's population serving the same God it would seem that historians would give more credibility to the history as recorded by these groups. The other religions are divided among the Asian countries, and to a lesser extent, the tribes of Africa and the Americas.

Unfortunately, to many people, the name of their religion is more important than what they believe! There are many 'religions' or beliefs in a God and the hereafter, and I believe that there is more in common among them than there are differences, similarities that we sometimes are unwilling to admit.

The Native Americans believed in the 'Great Spirit' and respected what they believed to be his will. Is that a separate religion from Judaism, also a belief in one supreme God? Most religions believe in a supreme intelligence that created us all. That belief is common throughout the world.

Buddhism is a philosophy, not a religion, if you define a religion as a set of beliefs that try to explain creation and a divine creator. Buddha was a man who never claimed divinity or a connection to anything divine. Buddha never advocated a belief that God did or didn't exist. He proposed a way of living and achieving inner peace and understanding of this life through natural means. Many people worship him. A religion doesn't worship man; it worships a God, or Gods, and tries to explain the hereafter. Anything else is a "philosophical body of thought".

Islam is a religion. It is very dedicated to a strong belief in one God and the law that He laid down for mankind. Islam descended from, and originated with Abraham and his son Ishmael by Hagar, who, according to *"Legends of the Bible"*, was the Egyptian servant girl who was given to Abraham as a gift by the Pharaoh who wanted Sarah as his own. It is also possible, according to the same document, that she was the daughter of Pharaoh.

All Islamic followers claim to be descendants of Abraham. They follow the same basic code of ethics and laws as the Hebrew code and have as their creation theory similar stories about Adam and Eve and Noah's Flood, as the Hebrew people. DNA analysis shows that the two peoples are virtually identical in their genetic make up. The difference is in their acceptance and definitions of some of the laws of God, and their belief in the stories concerning the prophet Mohammed.

Because the race of Islamic people was separated from the Hebrews before Moses, they do not have the laws given to Moses by God on Mt. Sinai as part of their code of conduct. Their religion followed a different branch and path from Abraham on, however in terms of their belief in God, and the creation of man, their system of beliefs is virtually identical to the Hebrews'. Their inspired document, that they say came directly from God through Mohammed the prophet, is the Koran, instead of the Torah of the Jews, and the Old and New Testament of the Christians.

What is the force that leads us away from the truth of our history and provides misinformation about who we are and where we are going? Why did man, who God cared so much for that he blessed him with gifts from the garden, in the beginning, not stay true to the one God? It seems that Noah would have handed down the historical record of how Man was saved from the flood by God and made sure that his descendants remembered and passed it on. Something happened to cause man to forget his creator.

Is it possible that just after the flood the ones chosen to carry God's gifts to the primitive tribes of Home sapiens throughout the world were so overcome by the adulation of the peoples they visited, that they began to believe that they really were Gods themselves? It has been shown many times that the act of putting a person in a position of extreme control and power over people corrupts the person by making him believe that he is superior to everyone else. "Absolute power corrupts absolutely". The Bible tells us that we should beware of such spiritual temptations.

Historical records tell us that the earliest leaders of Greece and Egypt *were* worshiped as Gods. It is hard to tell people that worship you as a God that there is another greater God. The temptation is to remain silent and let them believe what they want, as long as you are in power. I believe that the temptation and glory of being a God to these people prevented the further worship of the true God. Because of this, other religions and other Gods came to be worshiped throughout the world.

Is it possible that all "religions" that believe in a supreme being or creator, come together in the distant past, from one common origin that began in the Garden of Eden? If that premise is true then we should all celebrate our similarities and our common beginning, instead of believing, as science and the liberal media would have us believe, that the races of man and their various religions are all separate, unrelated events that happened randomly long ago in the distant unknowable past. Genesis chapter 10 is very specific in laying out the origins of the "Nations" after the flood and I believe that this refers to all peoples anywhere in the world.

At some time in the third millennium BC, it appears that men, descendants of Noah, visited all these lands and led their inhabitants out of the Neolithic age into civilization. By this action, and through their offspring, all races and peoples were re-created into a species that was far superior to what the science books refer to after the ice age as Homo sapiens. We are their progeny who carry their genetic contribution to mankind.

There must have been some effort to coordinate this vast project. There must have been some inner circle of administrators after Noah who, knowing what God wanted, sought to carry out His plan. There are historical records of such a project and even an administrator.

There is in the Sumerian texts, a reference to such a man named Ea who lived in Eridu, another city in Mesopotamia that was also mentioned in Genesis, in the third millennia BC, who was supposed to be the administrator over the dispersion of civilization and knowledge to mankind.

Hopefully future research will reveal more about individuals such as this, who remained true to God's will and was able to carry it out. They are the true heroes of our history. Without their efforts, where would we be today?

There are references in *"Legends of the Bible"* and Sumerian texts to a group of divine creatures called "The Watchers" who supposedly looked over mankind and his development after the flood. Are some of their group still around without our knowing?

After the flood and the establishment of Shumer, Noah's descendants were scattered to the winds to carry civilization to various parts of the world. It is strange that none of the nations mentioned in Genesis 10 became loyal to the God that created Adam but instead worshipped the "mortal" Gods that brought civilization to them. This practice established the various "religions" that came to be at that time. Only a very small line of people still followed and served the God of creation, those who came from the direct line of Shem and Eber, whose progeny eventually gave birth to the Hebrew people and Abraham. The word "Hebrew" is derived from the name Eber.

Why did God ask Abram to leave his country to go to the land "that he would show him" in Genesis 12? It would seem that God's plan from the beginning of the Garden project was to raise man up on two levels. One level would be in the area of intellectual and cultural accomplishments, to make man civilized and capable of learning, understanding, and appreciating the universe. Because of the "gifts" received from the garden as well as the training and expertise received from the "visitors" in each backward settlement, man has progressed in the arts, sciences, mathematics, and building skills until he has created a society that would, itself, seem as if "magic" to these ancient peoples.

Perhaps even more important than the first, the second level of advancement was for man to become moral. God wanted man to become a caring, compassionate, being, possessing emotions and characteristics that would not occur through natural selection, a man who would understand laws and the reasons for them, a man who could love Him and appreciate all that he had received from Him. Only a being with the "divine spark" of Adam would possess those qualities and would eventually be worthy of entry into the "Kingdom of God".

Someone had to preserve the truth of how God caused man to start on this journey toward civilization, technology, and understanding, and carry the message of "one God" to the rest of the world, a world that had abandoned him since Noah. It was through Shem's line down to Abraham that the message was preserved. From Isaac on, the descendants of Abraham lived lives not too different from modern man in terms of longevity and abilities. Abraham seems to have been the last descendant of Noah who still had the ability to directly communicate with God and enjoyed an unusually long life span. God evidently favored him by selecting him as the patriarch of a nation of people that He chose to carry on the story and the truth of how man developed after the Garden of Eden. Without this intervention by God through Abraham, and all that happened through his descendants afterward the story would have been lost forever.

When God asked Abraham to go to a different land He was isolating a specific line of the descendants of Adam and Noah for the purpose of creating a nation of people who could preserve the truth for the rest of the world to learn at a later time. 3.7 billion people who accept the stories as told in the Bible, the Torah, and the Koran are testimony to the success of this plan. God's efforts to preserve and bless this line from Abraham prevented the story from being lost to history. It was with Moses that He made final the plan to create the nation of people that would serve Him exclusively.

Chapter Sixteen

THE CASE FOR JESUS

In the book of Hebrews chapter 5, verse 6 in the New Testament is a cryptic phrase; "Thou art a priest forever, after the order of Melchisedec". The author was comparing Jesus to this man who lived in the time of Abraham. This passage is puzzling because Melchisedec was a priest just after the flood and the question has to be asked, "How was he relevant to this passage and what does it mean".

According to Frank Klassen in *The Chronology of The Bible*, Melchisedec was another name for Shem, one of the three sons of Noah. When the sons resettled and took their family to different parts of the world to begin nations, as described in Genesis chapter 10, Shem was the father of the Semite race and the Hebrew people. He ultimately settled southwest of the Mesopotamia region in the land of Canaan. Some think that he founded Jerusalem and the city was named for him, as in "Jeru Salem" or the city of peace.

At the time Abraham lived, Shem, or Melchisedec, was almost 600 years old and was the oldest living person on Earth, and was the last person to have seen the world before the flood. He was so revered that Abraham paid tithes to him. Since the bible has no mention of priests in the world before the flood, this would be a good time to ask. What is a priest?

Adam and his descendants had a peculiar ability that enabled them to communicate directly with God. Adam did it in the garden. Cain did it after his murder of Abel. Enoch and Noah did it at various times before the flood. Was this ability something that was inborn within them? We certainly know that no one today goes around talking to God orally in public, except during prayer, without his sanity being questioned?

After the flood, it appears that the ability to talk to God diminished until we get to Abraham, who apparently had the ability because he talked several times to God and to visiting angels. With the ability to talk to God fading the people who served God needed someone who still had that ability to speak in their behalf to God and ask for forgiveness for their sins. This necessitated the creation of the position of the priesthood.

Now we have a definition of a priest. A priest is someone who can communicate with God and relate the wishes of others to Him. Why some people can communicate with God better than others has always been a mystery. I would like to propose a theory and see if the theory can explain any other mysteries that may be outstanding.

We are today somewhat familiar with how DNA works to determine the genetic and physical makeup of any species of animal on this planet. When God created Adam he did so by designing a DNA strand that determined everything about him. We know now that by changing the sequence anywhere in that strand that we are changing the form of the creature that the DNA strand represents.

Suppose that there is a gene sequence in Adam's DNA that allows the ability to communicate directly with God. Suppose that this ability is still resident in our bodies today in a much weaker form, so weak that most of us are not even aware of its presence.

After the flood, this gene would have become weakened and diluted as each generation of Noah's descendants intermarried with the mortal man outside of Eden. Eventually, anyone who still had the ability in full strength as Shem did would be revered as a special person. People would come to him to learn God's will and to offer up their wishes. This is how the priesthood was formed.

Shem, or Melchisedec, was eventually the last living person who could talk directly to God. When he died, the gene in its original form and strength would never appear again in a normal man.

We have some strange accounts in the old testament of individuals born under unusual circumstances, apparently aided by an "Angel" who would come to a woman and announce to her that she would have a child who was to be dedicated to God his entire life. This happened several times. These individuals were known as Nazarenes and could never marry, cut their hair, drink strong drink, and would be dedicated to God's work for their entire lifetime. These individuals came to be known as prophets. Sampson, Samuel, Isaiah, Ezekiel, Elijah, Daniel, and Jeremiah were examples of these men.

It seems from time to time that God would intervene in the affairs of man to re-create a man with the abilities that had been lost since Adam and use him to lead the Hebrews back to Him. He would do this by using women who had no previous children and cause them to bear a child, even in old age. This had the effect of creating a man who had a new genetic structure that was closer to Adam's.

103

By repeating this act several times, generations apart, God was leading man on a path to a point in time when he would introduce him to a new concept. That concept would change the world for the next 2000 years. It's not surprising that the New Testament begins with such an act.

Not many Christians are aware of documents outside the Bible that tell of Mary's mother, Ann, who was one of those women who was advanced in age, barren, and prayed to God to give her a child. She was visited by an Angel who told her she would have a child. This time that child was not a son but was Mary, the mother of Jesus. This is the only recorded instance in which God used a woman in this way.

We all know the story of Mary being visited by the Angel Gabriel who announced that she would be the mother of the Messiah, from the book of Luke in the New Testament. What we have not given much thought to is the fact that Mary herself, born with only half the genes of mortal man, gave birth to a child who also had half the genes from his mother and the other half came from God. In this way Jesus was, as called by Paul, "the new Adam", because no human since the flood had possessed the purity of genetic structure that God had created in the Garden of Eden in Adam. In terms of genetic make-up He was actually ¾ divine and ¼ man, because half of his mother's genes came also from God.

Christ was the first human born since the flood who had all the genetic qualities of the descendents of Adam before the flood, of which Melchisedec was the last, born 2000 years previous.

If we look back to the time of Moses, the ability to communicate with God was practically non-existent for man when God called to Moses on Mt. Sinai and instructed him to create a priesthood from the tribe of Levi. Aaron was the first of these "mortal" priests. The ability to communicate with God was apparently no greater in these individuals than it was in anyone else, so how would they perform the responsibility of the priesthood?

God addressed the problem and told Moses how to make the Ark of the Covenant. It was designed as a box with certain characteristics as dictated to Moses by God, and would hold the sacred objects named in the Bible consisting of the Ten Commandments, some manna, and other artifacts.

How did it serve the priesthood? The Bible tells us that because it was dangerous to be around, it was sheltered in a place that was completely enclosed, called the "Holy of Holies". No one except the High Priest was allowed to enter this area. In fact, the act of entering a small area containing the Ark was so dangerous that the priest was required to wear bells that would jingle as he moved and so that outsiders would know that he was still alive, and tied a rope around him, to pull him out without having to go in and get him, if he were to die while in there. It is apparent from its placement and use that the Levite priests could only communicate with God while in its immediate vicinity, in the Holy of Holies. This suggests that it was a communication device.

Because a priest is supposed to relay communication between the people and God, how did he accomplish that feat without the ability that Adam had and was so weakened after Melchisedec, as to be ineffective? It seems very likely that the Ark was an object that performed that function in the absence of man's ability to do so.

One of the mysteries of the Old Testament about which books have been written and movies have been made is, what happened to the Ark. It was lost sometime after Solomon built the grand temple in Jerusalem and before the time that Judah was conquered by Babylon. It was not listed in a very complete list of articles taken from the temple by the Babylonians.

When the Jews returned to their homeland 70 years later they rebuilt the temple but without the Ark of the Covenant. It seems that the priesthood in those days offered only lip service to the people, as they were incapable of communicating with God, as had their forefathers.

When the angel Gabriel spoke to Mary and told her she would have a child of God she was overcome with fear and ran. On the second encounter with the angel she was put into a deep sleep while she was apparently made pregnant through artificial insemination by Gabriel. At that time Mary received half of the genes of Jesus Christ to join with her human genes to create a man like none other on this world, born both of God and at the same time, Man.

I believe Christ received much of the same genes that Adam had in the garden, but with so much more. He definitely had the ability to communicate directly with heaven and His Father. When he came into the world there existed for the first time in 2000 years, someone who could talk directly with God, anytime he wanted to.

Once again, man had a priest through which all his requests could be channeled to God. For the first time since Melchisedec, a man, Jesus, was able to communicate directly with God as had been done in the Garden, before the flood. We can finally understand fully Paul's expression; "Thou art a priest forever, after the order of Melchisedec

Chapter Seventeen

THE FINAL COUNTDOWN

It is my contention that the arguments presented in this book support my hypothesis that all those religions that accept a supreme being as our creator can trace their origins back to a common source. I would advocate that this belief applies even to the countries of the Far East and the Islands of the Pacific. There are myths and legends all over the world of beings of superior intelligence and abilities who helped and founded ancient civilizations. I believe that there is no place on Earth that did not receive at least some of the knowledge and fruits of the Garden of Eden after the dispersion at the Tower of Babel.

I strongly disagree with the anthropologists and scientists who like to categorize every unidentifiable artifact and finding they dig up, as being a "religious artifact", as if religion is something that is synonymous with superstition, and is inherent in man. This idea suggests that belief in a divine God had no origin except in man's ignorance and fears.

My experiences and beliefs tell me that man is not inherently religious and that the idea of a God or Supreme Being was a new and unique concept that began 6000 years ago. The media continually supports the scientific view of religion, as the newspapers and broadcast facilities try to dispel the idea of a divine entity. If the idea of religion is such a natural occurrence that is instinctive and inherent in man, why do so many college professors and media personnel find it extremely easy to accept and promote atheism?

I hope that in the preceding chapters I have presented arguments and supporting evidence that religion as a concept began on planet earth when beings who were visibly superior in intelligence and physical attributes to the other inhabitants, visited the primitive tribes and populations of Homo sapiens that lived 6000 years ago in much the same way that we send missionaries today to primitive tribes in central Africa, South America, and outback Australia to help them advance and learn better ways of living. It was through these visitors that the concept of "Gods" came to be. It was through a very special line of descendants, the Hebrew people, that the concept of one God who created and started Man's journey to a higher level of existence, was preserved, and that the story of the "true" origin of modern man began in the Garden of Eden.

It has been said that any sufficiently advanced technology will always seem to be "magic" to those who don't understand it. I have concluded that because of the reluctance of many in the scientific and academic community to consider the Bible as a source of information, they will continue to treat the "religious" version of creation as superstition and ignorance until sufficient advances in research determine what really happened during that unique and mysterious period of 4500 years ago that molded mankind forever, and gave us the tools to become a technological society. When those advances are made I am convinced that every word in the Bible will be found to be true.

I find that today my position is actually much easier to defend than it was 30 years ago. After the discovery of the so-called "mythical" cities of Ur, Nineveh, Nimrod, Sumer, Erech, and others turned out to not be mythical after all, they were found to have recorded histories that confirmed details about them that were seen previously only in the Bible. Before they became "fact" the scientific community regarded them as "religious myths". After the discovery of the clay tablets containing versions of some of the same stories, they responded that the Bible must have copied the stories from them. With the wealth of detail and other information contained in the Bible, it didn't occur to them that maybe it came first and was passed down by an oral tradition that predated even the Sumerians.

It was in the time period just after the flood, that a literal explosion of knowledge and civilization burst upon the world in a way that still baffles social and historical scientists today. It was also during this period that I believe that the religions of all the great societies were founded, based on the belief that descendants of Noah were Gods, because of their "differences" and abilities that were far above primitive Neolithic Man.

While scientists and academicians like to exclaim and pretend that they "deal only with facts and direct observations", it is only too obvious that much of what they publish as "fact", is still only an interpretation of what they have observed. They readily accept a story on a clay tablet about Gilgamesh as fact and reject a written account of Noah as myth, even though both stories refer to "the flood". What bothers me is that such learned men deliberately choose to ignore a source of information that can possibly help to explain what happened to bring man out of the darkness of the Stone Age.

There are several books and theories available that question what happened in the period between 2900 and 2200 BC to explain man's transition from the Neolithic age to the age of technology and civilization, and none of them give credit to a supreme being that created the universe. Why do I persist in believing that God was the force that intervened in man's development and advancement?

I like the answer given by the character Chantilas, in the movie "Red Planet". As one of the prominent scientists aboard the vessel sent to investigate life on Mars, he was asked why he believed in God. He replied, *"I realized that science couldn't answer any of the really interesting questions. So I turned to . . . God"*.

I, too, have spent a lifetime searching for answers to questions that I feel that science can never answer. I have come to believe there is only one answer for those questions, and that it is foolish to look in the physics of the universe for the creator of the universe. He does not reside in His creation any more than a painter resides in his painting. Such an entity would be truly eternal and timeless, but external to all that we call "the universe", and would of necessity be free of the restrictions of space and time that we hold so dear and necessary for anything to exist. Just as a famous line from another popular movie character advocates, "There can only be one".

The message is finally clear. We have been called by God to be more than human. Through a genetic signature that we received from Adam, we have all been chosen by God, and given the opportunity for a higher existence. We have the power to become a divine creature, as the Sons of God, spoken of by John in the New Testament. Some will hear the message and seek a higher level of existence, and some will revert back to the "primitive man" side of their genetic makeup, and refuse to acknowledge the existence of anything that we can't see, hear, or touch. The difference can be summed up in one word, a word that will seem foolish or nonexistent in the vocabulary of those who live by "survival of the fittest", FAITH. Some will have it, and some will not. I believe that difference will decide the ultimate destiny for each of us.

Reference Materials Used

In addition to sources mentioned in the text, the following materials were referenced in the writing of this document.

BOOKS:

E. A. Wallis Budge: *Legends of the Egyptian Gods* (1994)
James L. Kugel: *The Bible As It Was* (1997)
Colin McEvedy: *The Penguin Atlas of Ancient History* (1967)
Roy Willis: *World Mythology* (1993)
Frank R. Klassen: *The Chronology of the Bible* (1975)
Louis Ginzberg: *Legends of the Bible* (1992)
William Ryan and Walter Pitman: *Noah's Flood* (1998)
Erich Von Daniken: *Chariots of the Gods* (1968)
Irwin Ginsburgh: *First Man Then Adam* (1975)
Jerry Vardaman: *Archaeology and the Living Word* (1965)
David Fasold: *The Ark of Noah* (1988)
Charles E. Sellier & David W. Balsiger: *The Incredible Discovery of Noah's Ark* (1995)
The Book of Mormon (1981)
Ian Marshall and Danah Zohar, *Who's Afraid of Schrodinger's Cat* (1997)
Zacharia Sitchin: *The Stairway to Heaven* (1980)
Zacharia Sitchin: *The 12th Planet* (1976)
The World Bible Publishers, Inc. *The Lost Books Of The Bible, The Forgotten Books Of Eden* (1926,1927)
The Academy for Ancient Texts, www.ancienttexts.org, Timothy R. (Wolf) Carnahan, Founder; *The Epic of Gilgamesh (2004)*

MAGAZINE AND NEWSPAPER ARTICLES:

U. S. News and World Report: *Tracing Your Genetic Roots* (1/29/2001)
Time Magazine: *How Man Evolved* (8/23/99)

Discovering Archaeology: *The First European* (Dec. 2000)
National Geographic: *The Egyptians* (April, 2000)
Associated Press: *Gene Mutated in Fruit Flies Doubles Life Span* (12/2000)
Astronomy Magazine: *Egyptian Error Proves Pyramid Age* (March, 2001)

CPSIA information can be obtained at www.ICGtesting.com
Printed in the USA
LVOW05s1822051213

364050LV00002B/487/A